financial
FREEDOM
NOW

Max Edison

financial FREEDOM NOW

HOW TO WORK LESS AND LIVE MORE

PALADIN PRESS • BOULDER COLORADO

Also by Max Edison:

Beat the Bill Collector: How to Obtain Freedom from Your Debt

How to Haggle: Professional Secrets for Saving Money
    on Just About Anything

Financial Freedom Now:
    How to Work Less and Live More
by Max Edison

Copyright © 1999 by Max Edison
ISBN 1-58160-036-4
Printed in the United States of America

Published by Paladin Press, a division of
Paladin Enterprises, Inc.
Gunbarrel Tech Center
7077 Winchester Circle
Boulder, Colorado 80301 USA
+1.303.443.7250

Direct inquiries and/or orders to the above address.

Visit our Web site at www.paladin-press.com

CONTENTS

WARNING

The author, publisher, and distributors of this book do not advocate any illegal actions, nor are they engaged in rendering legal services or financial advice. The services of a professional are recommended if legal and/or financial advice or assistance is needed. The author, publisher, and distributors of this book disclaim any responsibility for personal loss or liability caused by the use or misuse of any information presented herein. This book is *for academic study only*.

CAVEAT

This is a book of financial advice, and, like most advice, it should be considered to be worth about what you paid for it. I consider the advice to be worth a helluva lot, which is why I spent a hundred hours or so putting it down on paper for you, but people who give advice always think that. It's possible that some of this information is dead wrong, though I'll bet you a hundred-to-one that it's not. It's also possible that laws, policies, etc., have changed between the time you're reading this and the time I wrote it. Not my fault.

In short, I did the best job I could in drawing you a road map to financial freedom. Please don't sue me if you get lost.

CHAPTER 1

FISCAL PARASITES

You're probably concerned about your money or you wouldn't be holding this book. Maybe you have so many bills that there's almost nothing left soon after you get paid—like you're getting up at dawn for two weeks just to get fifty bucks to call your own. Believe me, I know how you feel.

When I graduated from college and got out into the Real World, I was surprised to find out how much of my weekly paycheck was already spoken for. I'd work a 40-hour week and end up (after taxes) with a weekly wage of somewhere between $300 and $400. Out of that, I had to make any number of payments: truck, credit card, a line of credit at my bank, rent, groceries, insurance . . .

Well, I'm sure you know what I'm talking about. There were lines of creditors clamoring for my cash, and I knew they'd get ugly if I didn't keep 'em fed. I found myself doing work I didn't enjoy for what amounted to $50 or $100 a week, which was hardly an incentive to lock myself into a 40-year career.

Goddamn, I thought, *life as a grown-up has got to be more fun than this.* Remember what I was giving up: while in college, I'd have to get up early (eight or nine o'clock in the morning) perhaps four days a week. I didn't have to bathe or shave every day, I could wear T-shirts with pot leaves or obscenities to class, and I could go home and take a nap at three or four every afternoon. I generally took three-day weekends, too, either by skipping class or scheduling all of my classes so that my Fridays were free for sleeping in.

But I was always broke.

In the Real World, I found myself getting up at six o'clock in the bloody A.M., bathing and shaving every day, wearing an uncomfortable shirt and tie from the Salvation Army, and performing pointless work for eight hours a day. All around me, rejects from the *Dilbert* comic strip were speaking a strange sort of language, saying things like, "I want to shoot a concern at you," and "I want to be an eagle, not a duck." I watched mid-level management take perfectly good ideas like Continuously Improving Product Quality and Coaching (as opposed to Browbeating) and tack on so many riders and conditions that the original point was lost. Everybody seemed unhappy in these offices, shuffling around like extras from *Night of the Living Dead*, except that they were clamoring for coffee and doughnuts rather than brains.

And I was still broke.

Well, there was no way I was going to keep my sanity in places like *that* for more than a few months. I wanted to make money, sure, and I wanted to be able to support a family, maybe buy a house and take a few vacations. But not on those terms. I had to find out where the bulk of my paychecks were going, and fast. I needed to spend (or waste) less so that I could work less at a job I despised, or at least start building a big cushion so I could take a year off and get some writing done.

When I *truly* started paying attention to my money, I learned where it was going. And what I found out shocked the hell out of me.

When I started thinking about money full time and spent some time dealing with it in the collections and banking industries (as described in my first book, *Beat the Bill Collector: How to Obtain Freedom from Your Debt*), I started to see more and more ways that businesses, mostly large corporations, were siphoning money out of my pocket. Oh sure, it was all small amounts—five bucks here, ten bucks there—but when I added it all up, I was looking at $50 or $100 a month just in interest and service fees. That meant I was working five or ten hours a month to line someone else's pockets—at no benefit to myself.

And I was one of the lucky ones. I came out of college with only $500 or so in credit card debt, plus another $800 in a revolving credit line from my bank, plus a few thousand on a truck loan. A lot of my friends were carrying anywhere from *two to five thousand dollars* on their credit cards, *plus* new car loans, *plus* maybe a couple of grand for a computer loan. That meant they were losing as much as $2,400 or so, or working 240 hours *or more* (depending on what they got paid) per year just to pay *for interest* on their fancy stuff.

Now 240 hours is six weeks of work to you and me. Considering that the average person already works until almost the first of June just to pay federal, state, and local taxes, the remaining time in the year after that extra six weeks didn't leave a whole lot for food, rent, insurance, and beer, not to mention paying for those shiny new toys.

If that's the sort of fix you're in, this book will help. Maybe you make pretty good money but don't have anything saved up for emergencies or retirement. Nowadays it's pretty common for people to earn a million dollars or more during their prime work years, but if they're lucky enough to get the gold watch and the pat on the back, what have they got? Maybe twenty grand in the bank, a house, and Social Security. Pretty soon they're reduced to eating dog food and taking a job at McDonald's.

But what choice do you have? What choice does anybody have? That's the way things are, and unless your last name is Vanderbilt, you're stuck inside the system. Right?

Wrong. By following the directions in this book and starting to think carefully about your money, you can and will save hundreds, even thousands of dollars a year, dollars that you were formerly throwing away.

And those dollars equate to hours of your life, my friend. Ain't none of us gonna live forever, and every hour of your life you spend working to provide for your creditors is one hour you can't spend lying on the beach, playing with your kids, or drinking beer and hunting deer. If you don't get riled up thinking about someone else getting the benefit of your hard work, think about taking hours off your life and handing them to someone else.

It seemed to me (and still does, actually) that these banks, credit card outfits, rent-to-own stores, and other companies had taken a few lessons from nature. In the wild, the most successful parasites are the ones who take just enough from the host to survive and reproduce but don't take enough to kill it. These companies are economic parasites, pure and simple.

Skeptical? I can't say I blame you—I guess it sounds kind of paranoid, kind of like saying I believe the Bavarian Illuminati is controlling the monetary system, or the United Nations is just a front group for the Trilateralists. But read the book, let me build my case, and see if you don't agree.

$ $ $

In the next hundred pages or so, we'll be using some fancy lingo related to the world of finance. Some of these you'll undoubtedly have heard; others may be new. Here they are:

THE LINGO

401(k): An officially sanctioned retirement supplement (actually, for many people it's their main retirement savings) that's run through your employer. You kick in some bucks, he kicks in some bucks, and the whole mess is tax-deferred until you hit a certain age (currently 58 1/2 to 70 1/2).

Annual Fee: An annual fee is something you pay, like a membership fee, to a credit card company in order to have the convenience of being charged sky-high interest rates.

Appreciation: Appreciation may be loosely translated as, "Yo' shit be worth more."

APR: Stands for Annual Percentage Rate. When a bank compounds the money in a savings account or on a credit card, say, at 2 percent, the amount of money you receive (or owe) at the end of the year works out to be a slightly higher percentage rate than the one they're actually giving you. This is because of compounding, which means you earn interest (or owe interest) on previous interest credited (or debited) to your account. When advertising CD rates, banks always print the APR in big letters and the actual interest rate in small ones so the ad looks like you're getting a better rate than you actually are.

ATM: Automatic Teller Machines, otherwise known as no-armed bandits, are the short, squat machines that banks have installed in order to not have to talk to you. Perhaps this is a cynical view; ATMs do provide you with the ability to withdraw and deposit cash outside of normal business hours. They are probably responsible for at least half your overdrafts and possibly up to $20 or $30 dollars a month in bank fees.

Balance: The amount of money your bank says you have (versus the amount you think you have).

Bank: An organization normally housed within an imposing building. Banks borrow money from you (the depositor) in order to lend it to your neighbor (the borrower). Somewhere in this process, they make money, mainly by charging your neighbor 6 or 7 percent more than they're paying you.

Bank Card: As opposed to "department store card" or "gas card." In this book, "bank card" means a major credit card (Visa, MasterCard, Discover) issued by a bank. These cards can provide you with services or cash at a wide variety of locations rather than just at Amoco or Sears. You pay for the privilege.

Bankruptcy: A legal process whereby all of your debts are forgiven (commonly called Chapter 7) or where your payments are restructured to meet your budget (called Chapter 13). Once the scourge of the business class, bankruptcy has become popular in all walks of life. Since the number of declared bankruptcies keeps breaking new records, Congress will doubtless close currently available loopholes and scrap the current system. They have no choice: it's either that or the entire banking system goes piggledy-wiggledy.

Black: As in "In the . . ." not as in skin color. "In the black" basically means you're out of debt, making money. (See "Red")

Bounce: As in, "I bounced a check." This means you wrote a check for more money than the bank said you had in your account. If the bank chooses to cover it (they're not obligated to), the merchant you wrote the check to will get paid and be none the wiser. If they don't, you have to pay the bank's overdraft charge plus 20 bucks to the merchant plus the original amount of the check. Neat, huh? Don't you wish you owned a bank?

CD: Certificate of Deposit. CDs are kind of like a savings account, except they pay more interest and you can't pull your money out any time you like. You can buy them through your bank; be sure to watch for special rates.

Collateral: The stuff you have to ensure you'll pay a loan, besides your best intentions and honest face. If you get a car loan, for example, the car itself is usually owned by the bank, as collateral, until the loan is paid off. Awful nice of them to let you drive it while you're paying for it, though.

Collection Agency: Hired goons paid to call you up at inopportune moments and bug you for money. Do not confuse them with telemarketers, who are trying to get you into a position where you owe them money. With collection agencies, you already owe the money, and it's their job to wreck your day, every day, until it's paid.

Compound Interest: One of the best inventions of the 20th century, at least until credit card issuers got ahold of it. Say you want to borrow a hundred bucks from me for a year. Chump change, since I'm a famous author, but I'm no dummy—I charge interest. And I have a plan.

"Okay," I say, "but let's do it this way—every three months, I want to sit down and figure out how much interest I've earned so far. Then I want to add that to the amount you owe me and earn interest on that. Being gullible, you agree, and instead of owing, say, $106 at the end of a year (as you would with simple interest at 6 percent), you owe me $40,000. Just kidding. It's more than simple interest, but the difference doesn't get significant until we start talking about real money.

Credit: The ability to sucker somebody into believing that if they loan you money today, you'll pay them back Wednesday.

Credit Card: Also known as "plastic chains." Having credit cards comes from having the ability to sucker somebody into issuing you a card saying that you're a good guy and will pay your bills, and if you don't the issuer will cover you. Of course, this recommendation is not without compensation to the card issuer.

Credit Report: Imagine if all the people you've suckered into thinking you're a responsible citizen got together and exchanged opinions about you. That's exactly what a credit report is. It says who you paid, when you paid, how late you were, who's lending you money, and what the lender thinks of you.

Credit Reporting Agency: A firm that specializes in going around, asking your lenders what they think of you, and compiling their opinions into credit reports.

Debit Card: Like a credit card, except the lender doesn't trust you to pay him anything. Instead of floating you a line of credit like with a credit card, the lender instead allows you to spend money out of your checking or savings account, backed by the Visa or MasterCard logo (which ensures the merchant he will get paid). Touted by lenders as a better system than credit cards, but they lie.

Deductible: An accident penalty that you have to pay in the event you actually have to use your insurance. You get cheaper rates if you have a deductible of, say, $500. In exchange, you agree that if you ever have to file a claim with your insurance agency, you will pay to clean up the first $500 of damage. Since this naturally makes you more reluctant to report damage, this is a real winner for the insurance companies. Strangely enough, it can also be a real winner for you, as it cuts your insurance rates significantly.

Deductions (tax): Stuff the government recognizes that you might actually have had to pay for in order to live and continue to keep paying taxes. Strangely, rent is not deductible, nor is food, but phone calls made from your small business to your mistress are.

Depreciation: The government's dull-witted recognition that things are generally worth less money as they age and are used.

Escrow Account: An account at the bank where you store money to pay property taxes, insurance, etc., on your newly mortgaged home. Theoretically, this type of account is no-man's-land. In actuality, the bank owns it all. This term does not actually appear in this book, but my editor insisted I include it in the glossary anyway. Still beats working for a living.

FDIC: Federal Deposit Insurance Corporation, an entity that was instituted during the Great Depression to ensure that banks didn't close as often (kind of like an insurance agency for banks). Naturally, this works about as well as any other government program: the FDIC is broke after having bailed out its sister, the FSLIC

(Federal Savings & Loan Insurance Corporation), during the savings-and-loan scandal of the Bush administration, where presidential cronies got one-year prison sentences at Club Med after looting billions of dollars. Still, banks tout their (mandatory) coverage with the FDIC as though your money's as safe as God's kingdom. They lie.

Federal Reserve: Subject of much Internet paranoia, the Federal Reserve system was officially established on December 23, 1913. Each region of the country, as defined by the Federal Reserve, has one branch that handles check processing and cash supply for the banks of that region. The Fed (as it's familiarly known) is supposedly not part of the government at all, but a private corporation, in which one can supposedly buy stock. I haven't seen any prospectuses lately . . .

Financing: When ya ain't got the money, but ya gotta have something, that's where financing comes in. It usually costs you big. There are exceptions, however. If you borrow money to start a small business, then make huge profits at it, you're actually ahead. Why? Because without financing, you wouldn't even be in business. Financing is generally provided by banks, finance companies, loan sharks, and your dad.

Foreclosure: Remember back in "collateral," where I said that the bank actually owned the car until you'd paid off the loan? Foreclosure is what happens when you don't get around to paying off the loan. Foreclosure usually refers to houses and farms, but the term is technically correct when applied to any collateral. Basically, if you don't pay, the bank takes (or forecloses on) your collateral.

HUD: Department of Housing and Urban Development, a well-intentioned but bumbling department of the president's cabinet. HUD attempts to, among other things, raffle off condemned property, make it easier for families to buy homes, and construct housing projects such as those we've come to know and love in Los Angeles, New Jersey, and Washington, D.C.

Installment Loans: If you got a coupon book when you bought your new car, chances are you're paying on the installment plan. That is, you pay a little bit (sometimes a lot) each month, and eventually the loan is paid off. These are among the worst kinds of loans available, since it makes it easy for banks to charge you more interest in a variety of ways.

Insurance Premium: Truly a dorky term. "Premium" used to mean something good. Now it means "bill." It's what you pay every month when you bet that something bad will happen to you and the insurance company bets it won't.

Interest: What's the point of loaning money to someone (other than relatives) for years and not getting anything for your trouble? That's what bankers thought, and thus was born interest. Interest is a percentage of the original loan that you agree to pay in exchange for having the use of the money for a set period of time.

IRA: Stands for Individual Retirement Account. Kind of like a 401(k), but your boss isn't involved. You can start your own IRA at a bank or stockbroker's office and handle your retirement plans on your own. Best for people who are self-employed or work at places that don't offer 401(k)s.

Lien: Say you get sued. Say the person or organization that is suing you doesn't know how to get money out of you any other way but to slap down a piece of paper saying that if you sell your house or car, they have to get paid before you do. That piece of paper is called a lien. Generally, only banks or the IRS take this approach.

Liquid, liquidity: These terms refer to how easily you can pull your money out of investments, in cash. A savings account, say, is generally 100 percent liquid, meaning that you can show up at the bank on any given day, empty out your account, and take the proceeds home in cash or as a check. CDs, however, are not very liquid because if you take your money out before the CD becomes mature, the bank whacks you with an early withdrawal fee.

Money Market: The term "money market" in this book will refer to money market funds. Money market funds are 99 percent as safe as CDs, pay the same interest (roughly), and yet are 100 percent liquid. I've got one right now through American Express Financial Advisors that has no minimum balance and no service fees and from which I can write checks (over $100 only). Not too bad a deal.

Mortgage: A loan for a house. In the case of the 30-year mortgage, think of it as a way for the bank to help you pay for your house three or four times over before you actually own it.

Mutual Fund: Sort of "stock market lite." A mutual fund administrator buys shares of stocks, bonds, treasury bills, etc., organizes them into investment packages called mutual funds, and then sells you shares of whichever package or packages suit your financial needs. Probably less risky and easier in general for the average investor than picking individual stocks himself.

NSF: Bank-speak for "insufficient funds," or what happens when you write a check for more money than they say you have available. Contrary to what you might expect, banks love it when you do this, as long as you pay the resulting fees.

Overdraft: Means pretty much the same as NSF, though over-draft refers to the check you wrote and NSF refers to the type of fee you're getting charged.

Principle: The money you're loaning the bank (via a savings or checking account) or the money they're loaning you (as a mortgage or car loan). Interest is tacked on to this.

Rebate: A marketing gimmick used by manufacturers to sell more of their product. "Buy Flatline batteries and get 40 cents back!" and so on. To get a rebate, first you have to purchase the product, then assemble proofs-of-purchase, cash register receipts, and God knows what else and send it to East Corncob, Ohio. Wait six to twelve weeks and you get your forty cents back. Sometimes rebates are a very good deal; Sam's Club, for example, often adver-tises products that are free after rebate (you do have to pay sales tax, though).

Red: As in "in the red." This handy little phrase means you're spending more than you're earning—a fairly common state of affairs for today's Americans.

Refinance: If you're locked in a mortgage at, oh, 10 percent, and you wake up one morning and see that other lenders are offering 7 percent, it might make sense to refinance, or get a new loan at a lower rate to pay off the old one. If you've got a fair chunk of that house to pay off, you could save thousands of dollars by refinancing. Just watch the fine print.

Roth IRA: A new type of IRA recently given the green light by Congress. Whereas the old type of IRA (referred to by those in suits as "traditional IRAs") allowed you to deduct contributions from your taxes, then pay taxes on the money when you pulled it out, Roth IRAs kind of do the opposite.

You can't deduct contributions to a Roth IRA from your taxes, but once you've put money into a Roth IRA, you will never pay taxes on it again. Not when it earns interest, not when you pull it out. So the government says. Cynics among us will recognize that this could, of course, change whenever Uncle Sam decides he needs to fund some goofy project.

Social Security: A Ponzi scheme whereby today's workers pay for the living expenses of today's geezers, in the expectation that the workers themselves will pull in the bucks when they put on ugly clothes and head for sunny Florida. There are many problems associated with Social Security, not the least of which is the fact that today's Golden Agers are pulling much more money out of the system than they ever put in, even adjusted for inflation. When Baby Boomers trade in their BMWs and Merlot for walkers and Metamucil, the amount of people in the work force who'll be supporting them will be insufficient at today's tax rates. That is, we'll either have to come up with a bunch of workers out of thin air, or we'll have to tax each worker more. Or we'll have to cut SS benefits, which we won't, because old people have little better to do than write cranky letters to their Congressmen. At least that's what I'll be doing; I hate shuffleboard.

Bottom line: act like Social Security won't be around when you decide to retire. You may be pleasantly surprised, but then you may not.

Stock: Having a share of stock means that you own part of a corporation. If a corporation has net assets of $1.4 billion, and 5,000,000,000 shares of stock outstanding, and you own one share of stock, you have, well, diddly-squat. Hardly anyone ever buys stock because they want to build airplanes or run nursing homes. Almost everybody buys stock because they hope that at some future point they can get some sucker to pay more for it than they did. Much of the time they're wrong, unless they're investment brokers, in which case they can fob it off on their customers.

Tax Bracket: Instead of having a perfectly straightforward flat tax of, say, 15 percent for everyone, the federal government has decided it's fairer to punish the rich by taking a larger percentage of their money than, say, street mimes. Clearly a misguided sense of ethics.

At the time of this writing, your Adjusted Gross Income (what you made after the IRS lets you take some minor stuff off) will plunk you into one of five brackets: 15, 28, 31, 36, or 39.6 percent. Imagine you made $24,000 last year and $25,000 this year. We'll assume you filed as a single person, whether or not you are one. Last year you paid $3,600 in federal taxes, but since the upper cutoff for a single person is $24,650, you're going to be paying 15 percent of the first $24,650 and 28 percent of that last $350 this year, an extra 50 bucks or so. Understandably, penalties for jumping into a higher tax bracket get a lot bigger when you get to the country club set. That's why they work like hell to avoid it.

Taxes: A means whereby, under penalty of death, you are forced to gift some of the fruits of your labor to welfare cheats, crooked politicians, unwed mothers, sluggish bureaucrats, and hydroelectric dams for places like Phoenix, Arizona. America didn't have a permanent income tax until 1914, at which point the bill barely passed Congress. The rate was 1 percent, for everybody. My, how times have changed.

W-2: A form you receive from your employer each year. It states how much they paid you and how much they held back in the form of taxes (see above).

2

THOU
SHALT
CONSUME

Every day, you and I are bombarded with messages telling us to buy this, lease that, and borrow the other. Advertisements on TV and radio and those in magazines show us a world of glamour and excitement that we could become part of, and all it will cost us is $300 a month.

Obviously, everybody "knows" commercials lie. Nobody really expects to get blonde, bikini-wearing volleyball players free with the purchase of a case of Bud or to win every time they buy a lottery ticket. Still, the suggestion has been implanted. When in the course of our daily lives we run across a product that's been advertised, we tend to think, "What if this ticket *is* a million-dollar winner?" or "Please, God, let this truck be the thing I need to help me score big with the babes," or at least, "This soda is what cool people drink."

Thus, a product acts either as a genie, a magnet, or popularity in a can. Or so you hope. In reality, your odds of winning the lottery are ridiculously low, no strange women except hookers and cops are going to approach you in your truck, and soda pop is just vile sugar water in frighteningly unnatural colors.

Still, we go on buying. The economy, that all-important model of financial life—is nothing more than folks buying stuff from other folks. In order to be good consumers, and hence good little citizens, we're supposed to buy new junk like our lives depended on it.

Yet to a certain extent, they do. Say you work in a factory stamping out hubcaps all day. It's not a great job, not as good as being the president of a bank, but you need to keep it to pay the bills. Suppose people stopped buying new cars, which reduced the demand for new hubcaps. If the slump went on long enough, you might be laid off. Maybe the plant would even close.

If you were unemployed, you'd have to cut back on the stuff you could buy, possibly helping to make some other sap unemployed. And on it goes, until "our" government has to start a nice big war to pull us out of the economic slump.

In order to keep our jobs and make money, then, we have to buy other peoples' products so they have money to spend on the ones we produced, so we can pay for the stuff we bought from them and charged on our credit cards. Or that's the way the government's been telling us we ought to behave.

Frankly, I think there are some flaws in the government's logic. Personal indebtedness and bankruptcies are at all-time highs, savings accounts go begging for customers, tens of millions of Americans are on Prozac and other antidepressants, most two-parent households have both parents working and the kids in day care, and places like the Mall of America are considered major cultural icons. The important thing to ask yourself is, "Who benefits from this buying frenzy?"

The government, for one, since it gets a cut every time a buck changes hands. Corporations, obviously, since they're the ones selling all this junk, and, by extension, corporations' stockholders, since they profit as the corporation profits. And who are the stockholders? Why, millions of Americans just like you. Maybe even you. And, oh, foundations and other corporations, who are the largest stockholders. Their paper profits go on to benefit the government, and so on.

Maybe you own a fair amount of stock, say twenty grand worth. Even if you shop exclusively from the corporations that you hold stock in, your "kickback" is going to be so small as to be almost unmeasurable. So if you make a conscious decision to consume less and save more, it's not going to hurt your wallet any. Start letting everybody else pay the fat cats' green fees.

Almost everybody else is happy buying junk on credit and working to make other people rich. So don't worry about putting some schmuck out of work by changing your lifestyle—the only person who's going to notice a change in your spending habits is you. (By the way, in the event that this book sells 260 million copies in America, I apologize for single-handedly wrecking the economy. I'm just trying to make a living . . .)

But whether I wreck it or not, the economy is going to get worse. Don't get me wrong—I'm not trying to get rich by prophesying gloom and doom. What I'm telling you is a fact: what goes up must come down. The economy, like anything else, works on a cyclical basis, and soon enough interest rates and unemployment will go up, and the stock market will go down, further and more dramatically than it did in late 1998.

Even if you're happy carrying a heavy load of debt right now, even if you've got a great job and are making more money than you know what to do with, even if you've made tremendous paper profits in the market, I'm here to tell you that things won't always be so good. Better men than you have lost their jobs, through no fault of their own, and have been sent on their way with two weeks' severance pay and twenty minutes to clean out their desks. So don't you owe it to yourself and to your family to place yourself in a position to weather life's cruel jokes? You bet your life.

CHAPTER 3

GETTING STARTED

In any other book about personal finances, you'd be advised to keep a daily record of what you spend so you could see where all the money is going. That's a great idea, and I applaud anyone who can do it, but whenever I've tried such tactics, I fail. I keep excellent records for about three days, and that's where the experiment sits. Six months later, I stumble across the records while looking for the *TV Guide* and end up throwing the whole mess away.

Some plan. But even though money may run through your fingers like water, we're not really going to focus on your everyday purchases that much. I'm not going to hassle you about buying a can of soda every day to accompany your lunch, because you won't save a helluva lot of money by drinking water. Maybe $125 per year, if you buy it out of the machine at work, or $80 per year if you buy it by the case and bring it from home. Keep your soda pop if you want— it's a decision you have to make. What I want you to do is sit down and ask yourself if drinking pop with lunch is worth $125 a year to you. If so, drink and be merry.

I would ask you, though, to at least start paying attention to where your pocket money goes. You may find that a lot of it is going toward cheap junk that falls apart or loses your fancy in a few days. (Hey, relax. I'm sure you can get half a buck for that Mr. Spock coffee mug at your next garage sale.)

You might want to try an experiment: for one week, don't carry any cash. Leave your ATM card at home and force yourself to write checks for whatever you need. If you don't want the Mexican jumping beans from that attractive countertop display bad enough to write a check for them, don't get 'em. You know they'll be dead in a week anyway. No fair being sneaky and throwing them in with your gas purchase, either.

The big way we'll approach finances in this book is not by avoiding purchases, though. Rather, we'll be looking at things you'd pretty much have to pay for anyway and how you can get those products and services for as little dough as possible. We'll also be taking a look at different scammy products and services that various companies offer, and I'll explain to you why these things are rotten deals. Further, we'll be looking at what things cost you in the long run by figuring out what they cost you on a day-to-day or month-to-month basis, then multiplying to find out what they cost you per year.

What? Multiply? That's right, we're going to do some math. If you don't do the math, you may as well write "sucker" on your forehead and give all your money to the first huckster who comes along. The fact is, companies screw you on a day-to-day basis in the hopes that you won't do the math and therefore never look at the long-term cost. Usually, they're right.

Don't worry, we're not going to be doing quadratic equations. The level of math we're talking about here is really ninth-grade or below, the minimum most people should know anyway. If you're still apprehensive, there are a large number of "math made easy" books on the market; with a little diligence and ten bucks, you can learn to run the numbers like a pro.

Before we start saving you thousands of dollars per year (and hundreds of hours of your life), we need to figure out how much you actually make per hour. You may think you earn $10.57 per hour, or $75,000 per year or something, but you don't. The amount your employer *says* you earn includes taxes—money that is withheld from you by law and that, for the most part, will never touch your hands. Because your employer transfers the money directly to the government, it's never really "yours" according to any definition of ownership I've ever heard. (Sorry, just my hardcore Libertarian streak coming through there. I'll try to keep it under control in the future.)

To find out your actual rate of pay, dig into last year's tax returns. On your W-2 form, you will see the total amount you earned last year (the gross). Subtract what you paid in federal and state taxes and F.I.C.A. (also plainly listed on your W-2), then divide by the number of hours you worked last year (probably 50 weeks x 5 days x 8 hours, or 2,000 hours—I'm assuming you get two weeks of paid vacation per year or some other form of time off with pay). Now you've got your actual wage. Remember what this number is, because we're going to use it as a yardstick in the future.

Say you actually make $9.37 per hour. Whenever I quote a figure, divide that number by what you actually make per hour (in this case, $9.37), then ask yourself "Is this *really* worth _____ hours of my life?" (In this book, we'll use $10 per hour as your actual wage just because it's a nice, round number.)

It all goes back to putting things in perspective. Literally, time is money. Remember that your time is not unlimited, so you need to keep a sharp eye on how you spend it.

If you decide that a certain expense isn't worth X number of hours of your life, then you can have the happy (but, truthfully, not very exciting) experience of applying the money to your current debt and buying yourself time in the future, plus interest.

Think of it this way: if you're maxed out on a credit card with a $1,000 limit and an annual interest rate of 20 percent, you're paying $200 a year in interest really for nothing. If you keep making the minimum payment, say $15 every month, you're *never* going to pay the damn thing off, because 12 x 15 = 180. That is *less* than what you pay in interest every year. You'll keep chucking that money down a hole and going deeper every year to boot. To look at it another way, you'll be working 20 hours a year exclusively for the benefit of Citibank and its stockholders.

If you deny yourself a few luxuries, though, and pay the card off, you're saving yourself that 20 hours of work per year. You're buying your own freedom from wage slavery. Whatever you choose to do with this 20 hours a year is up to you—you could loaf in a hammock, or you could work anyway and use the money to open some sort of retirement savings account like an IRA. The important thing is that *you* are deciding how to spend your money—nobody's demanding the money, so you can do with it as you please.

CHAPTER 4

EASY
CREDIT

The fates work in mysterious ways. Right after I got done writing the last chapter, I checked my mail to see if anyone had sent me a big check. They hadn't, but what I did find was a credit card offer from someplace called Providian. Wait 'til you hear this:

The nice folks at Providian are writing to congratulate me on all the hard work I've done to pay my bills on time. They're happy to inform me that I qualify for a VISA Classic card with a credit limit of $400. It seems all I have to do to receive this card is send them a one-time processing fee of $89. They'll be happy to charge the $59 annual fee to my account when they mail me the card. Hmmm, it says here that the interest rate is a frugal 21.9 percent.

What they're telling me, then, is that all I have to do is send them a total of $148 for the privilege of borrowing money at 21.9 percent interest. Sign me up!

Obviously this is a terrible deal, but I seem to get about one of these applications per week. Apparently *someone* must be signing up with them or they wouldn't bother to keep bulk-mailing forms. The only thing more depressing than thinking about the poor saps who open accounts with this place and others like it is the fact that I myself probably would have done it at one point in the past.

In today's society, many people are so desperate to get credit that they'll join up with companies like Providian, bending over and dropping their pants just to have the opportunity to pay ridiculous interest on their purchases. (By the way, if you happen to have gotten screwed in a similar credit card deal, my heart goes out to you. Just don't do it again, and I won't feel compelled to tell anyone.)

The deal I got in the mail is perhaps an extreme example of how much credit cards can cost you. But it's not that extreme. Even a card that doesn't charge a processing fee can cost you quite a bit over the course of a year. Let's look at it: 18 to 23 percent interest on a $1,000 balance (and that's *compound* interest, folks, meaning that you pay interest not only on what you borrowed before but on the interest they've charged you so far this year and added to your balance), plus perhaps a $25 annual fee, plus two or three $15 late fees, plus three to five bucks a month for scammy card registration, disability insurance, and travel club deals . . . it all adds up. Then multiply that by the number of cards you have, which if you're an average consumer is five to seven, and we're talking about $1,500 or more per year just to carry those pieces of plastic in your wallet. Not smart.

Fortunately, credit is just a game, like anything else in the adult world, and there are ways to win at it.

My book *Beat the Bill Collector* has a pretty good insider's view of the credit game, but if someone broke into your house and stole your copy (nudge, nudge), I'll give you a brief rundown:

When I say the words "your credit," what I'm really talking about is your credit report, which is kept on file at any number of different credit reporting agencies. When you apply for anything from a credit card to a car loan, the company that considers giving you the loan pulls a copy of your credit report from one of these reporting agencies to see whether you're a good little wage slave or not.

What they'd really like to see on your credit report is the profile of someone who keeps fairly high loan and credit card balances, pays the minimum amount due every month, and could probably afford to pay a little more. The way they figure it, if you've got a little extra money each month, you could afford to pay it to them in interest. What lenders don't like to see is someone who has no credit or is chronically late with payments.

Well, people who've learned to value their financial freedom don't really like credit, because those interest charges put them into chains again. We do realize, however, that sometimes having good credit is necessary. Sometimes it's more convenient to order things over the phone, using a credit card, than it is to send in a check or money order and wait three weeks until it clears. Maybe we'll need to buy a house sometime in the future. Maybe the engine in the Chevy will seize up because we were too busy writing books to check the oil. And so on.

There are many ways to lose the credit game, but only one way to win—*by making sure that what you buy on credit doesn't cost you anything extra.*

Here's how to do everything right:

Step One: Those of you who have bad credit need to do more work than those who have no credit. You need to apply for a credit card and get turned down. When you receive the rejection letter in the mail, it will list the name, address, and phone number of the reporting agency who said you were a bad risk. Send a letter (certified mail, so they can't claim they never got it) to the agency requesting a copy of the credit report they have on you. You get one credit report free when you're turned down for credit; otherwise it costs about $15. See, you're saving money already! Your credit report will show up in your mailbox in a few weeks, along with (probably) a nifty set of instructions on how to understand what it's saying.

Look for those trouble spots. Maybe you had a credit card a few years ago, were late with payments, then paid it off when they shut down your credit line. Maybe it's an old doctor bill you never got around to paying. Maybe the agency just screwed up and put someone else's bad debt on your report (fairly common, believe me). Whatever the case, if an item is not currently in collections, you need to write back to the reporting agency and try to get it removed. You do this by, in many cases, lying.

Tell them you've never heard of Discover Card Services, and you certainly never had an account with them. Swear that the doctor bill was paid in full years ago. Be creative but not ridiculous; don't say you're with the CIA, or that space aliens were supposed to have taken care of your American Express card. Credit reporting agencies are authorized to discard any obviously ridiculous claims, so no matter how much fun it might be to tie the Kennedy assassination to your financial problems, don't do it.

Anyway, send them a letter outlining all of this stuff, send it certified mail, and wait. The agency will now have to contact the original lender to see if the record is valid or not. If the date of last activity on the debt is over three years ago, the chances are quite good that the original lender won't bother to verify it, in which case it will get removed from your record. Neat, huh?

Okay, so what happens if they *do* verify it? Well, then we start a war of attrition. You've got all the time in the world, so just keep sending those letters to the agency. If you get a couple of negative items removed but a few more are verified, send another letter. The agency will have to go back to the lender, and so on. Sooner or later, your verification will probably fall through the cracks and it'll get removed.

Sending your requests to the agency in the early summer and in November are probably the two best times of year to do it—hopefully when it arrives at the original lender, so many people will be off on summer or Christmas vacation that your request will get lost in the shuffle and will have to be removed. That's all there is to it.

Take note, however, that all items on your credit report must be removed seven years from the date of last activity (except for bankruptcies, which stay on for ten). That's federal law, folks, and woe betide the reporting agency who forgets it. If you've got a negative item on your report that is going to come off in six months anyway, it may be easier to just sit back and wait for it to disappear.

Federal law also allows you to attach a written statement of, I think, 100 words to your credit file. If you choose to take this option to explain a trouble spot, make sure the letter does you proud—don't rant about how Citibank had been gunning for you ever since you opened your account. I recommend blaming the whole thing on a dispute due to faulty record keeping on the part of the creditor.

Step Two: Start building yourself a good credit file by applying for the two easiest types of credit cards to get—gas station cards and department store cards. (Make sure to read the application carefully to avoid getting soaked with an annual fee.)

There are a few things to keep in mind to maximize your chances of getting accepted for credit: 1) Lenders like to give money to people who own, rather than rent, their homes because they think these people are less likely to duck out on their obligations. Plus, they like to think that they can slap a lien on your house if you don't pay, even though they hardly ever do. 2) Lenders like to see people who've been at their current jobs for a few (at least two) years. That makes them think you're less likely to switch jobs if they have to sue you and garnish your salary. As an aside, I should mention that lenders don't like to give money to unemployed or self-employed people. Claiming to be the great and famous writer Max Edison is probably not as good for your application as claiming to be a product polisher, third class, at the American Standard Urinal Company. 3) Credit card companies also like to see people who've been at their present address for several years. For some reason, they feel it's less likely that you'll move out in the middle of the night and flee to the workers' paradise of, well, Detroit or somewhere.

If you can find someone to cover for you, feel free to lie on your application. But be clever about it. If you just applied for credit at a different address six months ago, don't tell the lender you've been at your present address for ten years. Likewise with your job. Don't tell them that you make $70,000 per year as a sanitation engineer if you don't have a friend in personnel down at the city dump who'll back up your story.

For twenty bucks a month or so, you can rent a mail drop and a voice mail account to make your story seem more plausible. You know, something along the lines of, "Hello, this is Max Edison. I'm in a board meeting right now, but leave your name . . ."

Step Three: Once you get a card, use it to purchase stuff you'd end up buying anyway, like gas and laundry detergent. Remember to hang on to the money you'd otherwise be spending on this stuff; don't blow it on pull tabs. As a matter of fact, you can earn interest on it if you put it into your savings account until the bill shows up. When your bill arrives at the end of the month, pay it in full. Congratulations! You've just gotten an interest-free loan from Amoco and earned a little money at their expense! Now that's the way to beat the system.

Sometimes furniture stores, computer stores, and other places that sell expensive merchandise will advertise "no interest, no payments" for a year or 18 months. This is true, as far as it goes, but if you don't pay the balance due on the first payment date, you get socked for interest charges *retroactive* to the day you bought the stuff.

Say you buy a new computer from Lemon Electronics. The system you want is $2,000, or $2,130 after tax. They offer you financing and you take it. When your first payment comes due 12 months later, you make the minimum payment of $200. But as soon as Lemon Electronics gets your payment, they whack you with *a year's* interest at 18 percent because you didn't pay the whole balance when it was due. That's an extra $383.40 (actually a little more, since it's likely compound interest) tacked onto your bill before your payment is even processed. At ten bucks an hour, you're working almost a 40-hour week for the benefit of Lemon Electronics, and you still haven't made a dent in the actual purchase price of the computer. And did you notice that you're even paying interest on the *sales tax*, something from which you derive little (or no) benefit?

Now, how would a debt-free man handle this transaction? Well, there are a few different ways:

1) *Keep the money in savings until you're ready to buy, then pay cash.* (Good) This will ensure not only that you get interest on the money while it's sitting in the bank, but you're less likely to make an "impulse buy." While building up your bankroll, you'll have a chance to check out other retailers and wholesale-by-mail dealers for the item you want (possibly saving yourself the sales tax to boot).
2) *Build up the money in savings, take the "interest free for a year" deal, and put your money in a 12-month CD or money market account.* (Better) Now you're earning more interest while building the bankroll *and* getting a 12-month interest-free loan at Lemon's expense.
3) *Buy a six-month-old system from a pawnshop or private party for half of retail.* (Best) Even though you're not getting an interest-

free loan, you're getting what is essentially a new computer for half price, thus saving $1,000. If you buy from a private party, of course, you even avoid the sales tax. You've just saved yourself almost three weeks of work *and* gotten your computer.

There are always loopholes; finding the best one can really pay off. Now, back to building your credit.

Step Four: Once word gets around that you pay your bills regularly, you'll be besieged with applications for VISA, MasterCard, Discover, and American Express (bank cards). Now you can think about getting a couple of these bank cards to further help build your credit. Just remember to hold out for the cards that don't charge an annual fee, have reasonable interest rates (not like you'll ever end up paying interest charges, right?), and maybe send you a year-end check for a couple percent of the total amount you spent with their card that year.

A word of caution: sometimes a bank card will offer a "no annual fee" deal for the first year only or will try to add one after you've been with them for awhile. Don't put up with these scams. Let someone else pay for their stock dividends. Tell their customer service rep (or, preferably, customer service *manager*) that unless they knock off the song-and-dance about annual fees, you'll be closing your account. If they won't waive the fee, keep your word and close it. If you currently have a card that charges an annual fee and have been good at paying it for the past couple of years, you can try the same deal. Credit card issuers will frequently waive the fee rather than lose a customer.

Step Five: Treat bank cards exactly as you did department store cards. Use them *only* to buy stuff you'd otherwise purchase (groceries, etc.), keep the same amount of cash in your savings account, and pay the balance in full when the bill comes at the end of the month. Bank cards generally charge an extra 2 to 5 percent service charge for cash advances, so read the literature carefully, and don't take cash advances unless they're "free." You may be tempted to let the balance on one or more of your cards slide for a month in certain cases—don't.

If you don't listen to anything I say in the rest of the book, listen to this: it's amazingly easy to let your balance slide for a month, two months, six months. Then they've got you—you've just lost the credit game. One day you're going to wake up with $6,000 in credit card debt and you'll be a wage slave again.

Think of it this way: every time you charge something on your card, it's just like going into your local bank, sitting down with a loan officer, and signing papers on a loan at 21 percent. No sane person would pay that kind of interest if they had to actually go in and apply for a loan, but it's all too easy just to whip out that plastic and do exactly that! Guard your freedom zealously, because it's easy to let it slip away. I speak from experience.

In addition to annual fees and sky-high interest rates, bank card issuers make their money by offering various programs and memberships that you can pay for. These include a credit registration service (in case your wallet is lost or stolen, you can call one number and get all your cards canceled), travel clubs (which offer discount air fares), and insurance plans to pay your credit card bills in the event you should ever become disabled or dead.

These programs, almost without exception, are junk. They're ways to chisel a few more bucks out of you each and every month. For example, while credit card companies try to play on your fear of some thief running into Bloomingdale's and racking up your card, federal law says you're only responsible for the first $50 that an unauthorized person charges *before* you notify the credit card company. Everything that happens after that is at no cost to you.

Now you may be thinking, "Yeah, but I've got five credit cards— that's $250." True, but when's the last time you actually lost your wallet? It was ten years ago for me, and all that was in it was an ATM card and some receipts. And even though these card issuers are offering to *register* your cards, they may or may not be offering to pay the $50 per card charge for you. Your best bet is to keep a list at home of all of your card issuers, their phone numbers, and your card numbers. When and if the worst happens, you'll have one place to go to cancel all your cards. You'll also be saving yourself at least $25 (two-and-a-half hours of work) per year.

If a card comes with free benefits, by all means sign up for them, but only if the card itself is a good deal. If you wouldn't apply for a Gotrocks Bank card without the travel club, don't sign up for it just to get the travel club. You're better off checking out travel rates on the Internet anyway.

And about that disability insurance: basically, these policies supposedly ensure that if you die or your legs fall off or something, your credit card bills will be paid, thus preserving your fine credit rating. I don't know why anyone would worry about paying credit card bills after they're dead, but in any case, isn't that what life insurance is for? Personally, I think that if I was dead or disabled, I'd just go bankrupt, but if you're going to lay around nights and worry about making your VISA payment, rest easy. You can buy disability insurance from a local insurance agent for a much lower price (comparatively speaking) than you can through your credit card company.

Here's the biggest way you get cheated by purchasing life and disability insurance through your credit card company: the insurance will only pay for the outstanding balance of the loan. If you get disability insurance from State Farm or somebody, the policy will generally state a certain dollar amount, like $20,000 or $50,000. If you sign up for a policy from a credit card company or a bank, however, you're only covered for what you currently owe them. You may be paying the same insurance premiums for $1,000 worth of coverage or less.

Sometimes credit cards (like Discover) will come with blank checks you can write out on your credit account. Often these checks will have no added fees; that is, while a cash advance from an ATM might cost you 2 percent immediately, writing a check for cash shows up just like a regular charge—no interest fees if you pay the balance every month. It's obviously in your best interest, then, to write the check out to your bank to the maximum amount of your credit and deposit that money in savings for a month. At the end of the month, pull the money back out, pay your balance in full, then repeat the process.

The funny thing is, the more you do this, the more the credit card company thinks you're a big spender and the more likely they are to increase your credit limit. At the end of a year, you'll not only have all the interest you earned on someone else's money but you'll get a check from Discover for 1 percent or so of the amount you "spent" that year. Let's find out how much that rebate check would be:

Discover often starts people out with credit limits of, say, $1,500. So 1,500 x 12 months is $18,000. One percent of that is $180, or 18 hours of work you didn't have to do. Add that to the $30 or so you get from interest by putting the money in a savings account (could be higher; I calculated it at 2 percent APR since interest rates for savings accounts are in the dumper right now) and you've got $210, or better than half a week's paid vacation. Not too bad a deal, huh?

I should mention that the only exception to using the charge-stuff-and-earn-interest-on-the-money scheme is when you can negotiate an instant rebate for yourself. You see, not only are credit card companies nickel-and-diming you, they also soak the merchant for 2 to 5 percent of your purchase every time you use your card. Merchants know this (obviously) and price their merchandise a couple percent higher so they're really not losing any money if you charge your purchase.

Well, now that you know that, and you know the merchant knows it, what's the harm in trying to get a cash discount?

Tell the store owner or manager (not the sales rep or the clerk at the counter) that you'd like to buy his lovely stereo but you were wondering if he could give you a discount for cash. About one time in three, he'll say yes. Now, instead of getting 1/12 of, say, 2 percent from your bank, you've gotten a 2 to 3 percent immediate discount on your purchase. I know, I know, it seems like chump change, but it all adds up.

This trick, by the way, seems to work better at stores where the guy behind the counter is the owner rather than at chain or department stores. Your purchase of a new refrigerator from Joe's OK Appliances might make Joe's car payment that month. At Best Buy or Sears, however, you're just another entry on a ledger, and the store manager probably won't lose much sleep if you decide to take your money down the street.

Step Six: Now that you've built yourself a good credit rating, it should be a snap to get bank loans. Bank loans differ from credit cards in that interest on the money you're borrowing starts to accumulate the first day, generally speaking. Thus, tucking the money in savings won't work. You'll be earning 2 percent on the money and paying 10 percent, for a net loss of 8 percent. Not smart.

Auto loans are among the easiest types of loans to get, basically because the car is your collateral. You've probably seen ads for cars in your local paper that proclaim, "Your Job Is Your Credit," and so on. These dealers generally go through finance companies rather than banks, so the interest cost is higher. There are a few problems with getting a loan to buy a car:

1) You have to pay full-coverage insurance on the car until the loan is paid off, even if it's only worth a couple of thousand dollars. As a matter of fact, anything you put up for collateral for a bank loan is going to have to be insured, be it a car, house, boat, or whatever. While this is as much for your benefit as the lender's (imagine making $200 or $300 payments every month on a car that was towed and crushed months ago), it's an added expense that you should take into consideration. The Nissan Sentra may not be as much fun to drive as the Saab 900 Turbo SPG, but unless you're James Bond, the cheaper insurance tag on the Nissan will give you a couple more hours of freedom each month. Heck, real spies like CIA agents drive around in Ford sedans, so get one of those if your job is to make the world safe for democracy.

2) Every car depreciates every day. New cars can lose thousands of dollars of value the instant you drive them out of the lot. You don't want to be stuck taking that kind of loss *and* paying interest on it. Financial Freemen never take out loans for things they *know* are going to depreciate—it's like getting shafted twice on one set of paperwork.

   There are plenty of books available about getting the best deal when buying a car, but you might want to consider a car that *looks* new but which has several thousand miles on it. My grandma Harriet got a Chrysler Behemoth that had been used by a Chrysler exec for a year; it only had about 12,000 miles on it, it was still covered by the factory warranty, and she paid five or six thousand dollars less than getting a new one of the same model. No, it's not new, but it's a savings of three months at hard labor.

3) It's a lot easier to get more car than you need when you think about your purchase in terms of "only $299 per month" rather than $8,000 plus tax, license, and registration. So when you're thinking about buying a new or used car, don't think about the monthly payment. Think about writing out a check for $30,000 or whatever the purchase price is. Think about how many hours you'd have to work before you own it. If you're like me, it'll be pretty difficult to even imagine whipping out the checkbook for a brand-new car. Like the guys on "Car Talk" say, "Is a brand-new Mercedes *really* $68,000 better than my Dodge Dart?" Chances are, it's not.

The biggest bank loan (we were talking about bank loans, if you'll remember, before I started rambling on about insurance and depreciation several paragraphs ago) you're ever likely to get is a mortgage, and it should come as no surprise that banks have engineered more ways to screw you through your mortgage than through any other activity.

In fact, banks have come up with so many ways to screw you *in general* that I'm going to devote two whole chapters to beating your bank.

CHAPTER 5

BANK ROBBERY

No institution, save the government, has figured out as many ways of separating you from your money as banks have. Most banks look like trustworthy, solid institutions, with their imposing Greek-pillared facades and their impressive-looking rent-a-cops. But just inside the doors lies a den of well-dressed thieves.

Banks figured out the concept of screwing you by the penny, rather than the dollar, long ago. Remember—like a parasite, they want to bleed you, the host, for as long as they can without killing you. On something as simple as a savings account, you might find several different ways to lose money: ATM fees, under minimum balance fees, withdrawal fees. Heck, some banks are even charging a fee to deal with a live teller. Checking accounts are even worse: add overdraft (insufficient funds, or "NSF"), per-check, and check printing fees to the previous list.

Unfortunately, a checking and/or savings account is something of a necessity in today's world. Therefore, it pays to take a look at what banks do, then figure out how to beat them at their own game.

First of all, there's nothing a bank loves more than someone who bounces checks—that is, as long as that person pays for them. Even though they may sound gravely concerned when you bounce one, like you're a disobedient child or something, they'll secretly love you for it.

When I worked in the customer service department at TCF Bank in Minneapolis, my supervisor told me that her willingness to haggle with a customer depended on how many checks he'd bounced in the past year. If someone had bounced 20 or more, she'd do almost anything to make sure he stayed with TCF, as he had proved himself to be a reliable source of revenue.

How much does it cost TCF when one of their customers bounces a check? About a buck, counting labor and lost interest on the money. How much do they charge their customers? Twenty-four bucks. Assuming that it takes you a week to pay the bounce fee, the bank is getting a 1,248 percent return on their money (24 x 52). Quite the return on their investment, I must say.

But banks have the most fun when one of your overdrafts triggers a string of others. As far as I know, banks don't make a special effort to send the biggest checks through first. As a matter of fact, TCF credits all deposits to accounts before subtracting debits. Nevertheless, whenever a whole string of checks bounce, it seems like it's always one big one, then a slug of two- and three-dollar ones. Naturally you get charged for each of them. Okay, to be fair, some banks have a maximum-fees-per-day policy, where they only charge you for up to five NSFs per day or so. Still, that's $120.

Of course, banks are not at all obligated to cover an overdraft. If they don't cover a bad check, *you* get popped the $24 or whatever, *plus* whatever your state says the merchant can charge you. Space constraints and sheer laziness prevent me from giving a state-by-state listing, but here in Minnesota it's 20 bucks. Often there will be a sticker on the cash register at your grocery store or whatever that states the extra amount that the merchant can tack on if you bounce a check at their establishment.

But not only do banks make money when you bounce a check, they also make money when someone deposits a bad check you wrote them. All they do is charge another fee to the people who deposited the check. If they get lucky, the people who deposited your bum check will write checks on *it*, resulting in yet another bunch of fees. Oh, I'd *love* to run a bank—they've got the traffic coming and going, and they rarely fail to collect their fees.

You see, most banks subscribe to services which are kind of like a credit reporting agencies for checking accounts. If you've had an account closed at another bank because you didn't pay for your bounced checks (or the fees that resulted), this service will make it well-nigh impossible for you to get a checking account at any other subscribing bank for several years. That, plus your old bank will be calling and hammering on you for the money you owe them.

Banks are so fond of overdraft fees, as a matter of fact, that they've come out with a couple of new products to help generate more of them. One is the ATM card, which, unless you've been living in a 9 by 12 shack in Montana for the past 15 years, you know allows you to pull money out of your bank account at casinos, bars, and other financially perilous locations. The other is an expanded form of the ATM card that features a VISA or MasterCard logo. These expanded ATM cards are marketed under different names, like US Bank's (formerly First Bank) Chextra or TCF's Check Card, but they're commonly known as "debit cards." Debit cards not only allow you to withdraw money via an ATM but to electronically transfer money from your bank account to the merchant or Internet porn site you'd like to pay.

Banks have found that these two products are just so darn convenient for their customers to use that their customers often forget to write down cash withdrawals or charges made on them. In fact, when I worked in TCF customer service, I found that the vast majority of overdraft charges were due to customers forgetting to write down ATM and debit card transactions.

Are these two products convenient? You bet. Are they dangerous? You bet. I recently caught myself forgetting to write down transactions with my debit card, and you'd think that I of all people would know better.

And then there are the other charges—under minimum balance fees, at some banks, maybe per-check fees, sometimes even a fee for depositing items into your checking account. There's also an unavailable funds fee, which is triggered when you deposit a check from a faraway land into your account, then try to write checks against it. If it seems like they've got you almost no matter what you do, you're catching on to the bank game.

Here are some tips on how to keep your financial freedom:

- Shop around until you find a bank that offers the best deal on checking. If I have to have a bank account, I want my bank to lose money on me. I currently have an account with no monthly service fee, no minimum balance, no ATM fees (as long as I use ATMs owned by the bank, which you can bet I do), no per-check charge, and no charge per deposited item. All I pay for (assuming I do my math correctly and don't bounce any checks) is check printing, and I even got my first box free when I opened my account rather than taking the 10-piece Tupperware set they were offering at the time.

    I have what is called "Totally Free Checking" with TCF, and as long as you do everything right, it really is totally free. No, I'm not taking any money for this plug. This account is a good deal *if* you do everything right. If there's not a TCF near you, do some shopping around before you open an account and see what's available. It may take you two or three hours to sift through all the information, but the money you save will add up over time.

- If your credit is good (which it should be, sooner or later, if you followed the instructions in the last chapter), I highly recommend that you apply for some form of overdraft protection from the bank where you have your checking account. Overdraft protection is basically a line of credit that kicks in when a check, charge, or withdrawal would take your checking account into the red. Money is advanced into your account from the line of credit, enabling you to avoid a nasty overdraft fee. We all make mistakes from time to time, and though overdraft protection loans are generally at 18 percent, the interest you pay is a helluva lot cheaper than getting smacked for $24 or $44 for each check you bounce. There's generally no fee for these services besides the interest, and you can usually pay them off at any time without a penalty.

- I would recommend that you do not apply for a debit card unless you are unable to get a credit card and feel you need the convenience of being able to order products over the phone, open an account at a video store, or whatever. There are so many different ways that a debit card can help overdraw your account that they're really not worth the risk. On a credit card, these mistakes would be minor nuisances, but with a debit card, each mistake could trigger an avalanche of hefty NSF fees because every time you use the card, it withdraws cash from your account just as a check or ATM withdrawal would. Here are some of the things that could (and frequently do) happen:

1) You could forget to write down the transaction and thus bounce a string of checks.

2) It's horribly likely that a company to which you return merchandise will forget to (or take their sweet time to) credit the purchase price back to your account, leading to, well, you know. Even if you get things squared with the store, the bank sees it as your fault, and you're still stuck with the fees resulting from the misunderstanding.

3) A merchant could mis-key the information when running your card through the little gray box, thus turning a purchase of $8.89 into $88.89. Again, you'll probably be stuck with the resulting NSF fees after everything's been straightened out.

4) Sometimes places like hotels will put several-hundred-dollar "holds" on your account until they make sure you didn't walk off with the TV. Sometimes they won't tell you that they're doing so just because the clerk has his own problems and doesn't give a damn about you. Unless you can get them to pay your NSF charges, which is unlikely, you'll be stuck with the fees.

5) Knowing how frequently retail clerks check I.D. when processing a credit card purchase (virtually never), a thief could drain your checking account in a matter of minutes just by running around in the mall and going on a shopping spree. Sure, you'll get the money back, but only after several weeks pass and dozens of reports get filled out.

I actually wrote "ask to see I.D." on the back of my debit and credit cards—about one clerk in five ever bothers to check.

- Do not, unless absolutely necessary, authorize direct withdrawal from your checking account to pay utility bills or insurance or to transfer funds to another account. These automatic payment plans are efficient NSF generators. Not only might you forget that a payment is due to come out, but discontinuing these withdrawals seems to sometimes be a real problem.

  If you're paying dues to a health club through automatic withdrawal, for example, and want to drop your membership, it may take several phone calls and a couple of months before your request gets pushed through their bureaucracy, which means you're still paying for a gym you no longer use.

  Pay your bills the old-fashioned way, by sending off a check (or at least claiming to). If you have checking with interest, you'll earn money while the check waits to clear. Automatic payment doesn't look so convenient when it costs you a couple hours of labor to pay for the resulting NSF fees that often result.

- Likewise, I would avoid allowing anyone to deposit money automatically into your account. In addition to the headaches that result from changing accounts or banks (i.e., your company's payroll department can't figure out which account gets the money), there's a very real danger that you almost never hear about: once you give someone permission to put money *into* your account, you also (unwittingly) give them permission to take money *out*.

  Say you work for Stinky's Flowers. Your paychecks get automatically deposited to your account. You quit one day, because they obviously don't recognize your value as an autonomous human being. Two years later, Stinky's conducts an internal audit and determines that they overpaid you by $500. They pull the money out of your account, and you bounce five or 10 checks. You pay your bank big bucks for the resulting NSFs. All perfectly legal; I've seen it happen.

- If you do screw up and bounce a check, banks will often reverse (that is, get rid of) one or more of the fees you've racked up. You may have to talk to a supervisor to get the job done, as in my experience the "front line troops" of customer service take pride in turning down requests like this, but it does happen, and quite frequently.

  My friend Dan once had three checks bounce on the same day, and he kept calling TCF's customer service line to get at least some of the charges reversed. They flatly refused. He called me and I reassured him that they certainly would do such a thing and told him to ask for a particular supervisor by name the next time he called. He ended up getting $48 of the $72 in fees reversed.

  The rule of thumb we used at the time was that generally no more than half of a particular day's fees would be reversed, so Dan really got a good deal. Of course, he was still paying $24 for a three-day loan from TCF, so maybe it wasn't all that great a deal.

  It used to be a matter of pride among us "customer service" reps to dig in our heels and not reverse any more fees than we absolutely had to. In retrospect, I don't even see any reason for that attitude—it's not like we were getting commission or anything. More than once I refused to reverse any charges for a customer who had bounced four or five checks in a day, giving them some hogwash line about them having to establish a positive balance in their account before I could do so. In effect, I just tried putting them off repeatedly, hoping they'd forget about it. If you bounce a check, or if your bank account comes with service charges that you were not made aware of, feel free to lean on your bank for a fee reversal. Just keep going up the chain of command until you find someone who'll make you happy.

- Never send off a check before you've got the money in your account. I know this sounds like a no-brainer, but you'd be surprised how fast a check can whiz through the system. You figure maybe two days in the mail, two days to get through the Federal Reserve clearing system, and you're set, but I've seen checks I've mailed come through on the third day. You may be thinking,

"Well, geez, I'll get socked with a late fee if I don't mail in that payment to my credit card *today*." Well, maybe so, but would you rather pay a fine of 10 or 24 bucks?

- If you have checking with interest, which you really should sooner or later, send your bills off on the last possible day. Legally, if your payment is postmarked on the due date, that's the same as walking down to the power company or wherever and paying in person on that day. This gives you an extra couple of days of interest. Hey, it seems like chump change, but it all adds up. Banks make their money by the penny, too.

- One clever trick for avoiding overdrafts, which I would like to think that I discovered, is to round all debits and checks *up* when recording them in your check register and round all deposits *down*. Even accountants have been known to bounce checks; this method helps build up a hidden reserve in your checkbook that may save your butt. Of course if you choose to use this system, you can't expect your balance to agree with the bank's when you look at your statement. It seems like it never does, anyway. Just ignore what they say you have in the bank (unless it's a lot less than what you think you have) and mark off the items that have cleared.

- Never write postdated checks. Used-car dealers and all sorts of other folks will swear up and down that they won't put the check in before the date written on it, but they lie. Or they make mistakes. Again, you get stuck with the fees, unless you can get them to reimburse you.

  The only place you can write a postdated check and know that they won't cash it before the date written on it is collection agencies, which are prohibited by federal law from doing so. Other than that, I wouldn't even give a postdated check to my mother. Contrary to popular wisdom, banks don't care at all about the date written on the check, and they'll attempt to cash anything presented to them.

- Sometimes banks like to hang on to a check you deposit for up to five "business days" (which, during the holiday season, could end up being a week and a half as normal human beings reckon time). Say you deposit a check for $5,000 from your insurance company, and you want to buy a new(er) car. If you go down to the lot and pick yourself out a cream puff the day after you deposit the check, the chances are good that your check for the car will bounce, especially if your insurance company's check is from out of state. And if your check bounces, of course, you incur a service charge *plus* the wrath of Happy Larry's Discount Cars. That wrath may add up to 20 bucks in a bounced-check fee, or it may add up to a criminal charge of "issuance of worthless check," which could land you in jail, theoretically.

The standard explanation for this hold goes something like this:

"Sir, we clearly post a funds-availability schedule in our lobby which clearly states that nonlocal, nongovernment checks may take up to five business days to be credited to your account." What the service rep means when she says this is: "Okay, you came down to the bank yesterday and deposited your check. You think that check was money, but really it's not. All it is is a promise to pay you some money. We've got to go all the way down to Georgia (or wherever) and collect that money for you, and that takes time. Now we don't mind floating you a loan on some of it—you're not going to get evicted or starve to death because we're en route to Georgia—but we really can't loan you the whole five grand, just in case it's no good."

That's the explanation that I used to give TCF customers when they called up, hopping mad, because their check bounced.

You may be happy to know, however, that there is a way around this hassle: deposit your money through an ATM. According to federal law, deposits made at ATMs must be credited on the second business day after the deposit. If your bank, for example, credits all deposits after 8 P.M. (like TCF does) and you deposit your out-of-state check before 8 P.M. on, say, Monday, all of your money will be available on Wednesday. It may not be instant cash, but it beats sitting around for five business days and/or getting socked for "unavailable funds" fees *plus* whatever the merchant might stick you with.

• If you end up getting stuck with a checking or savings account that requires a minimum balance (more and more common in these hard times), I recommend that you deposit the minimum balance, then forget about it. Most such accounts are set up so that if you dip below the balance even once during any given month, you get socked for $5 or so, which in the case of a savings or checking-with-interest account negates several months to a year's worth of interest. If the minimum balance is, say, $300, put your $300 into the account and record it in your register as "$0." This will help you avoid getting screwed, unless you get clever and try to access your hidden balance in an emergency.

• Don't get suckered in to buying fancy checks. Frankly, no one but you cares what your checks look like, and if you define yourself by the pictures and snazzy writing on your checks, you need to get out of the house more often. Ask yourself whether you'd rather have checks with Bugs Bunny on them or two more hours of freedom every six months or so. It all adds up.

    If you absolutely *must* have Bugs and Porky on your checks, place your order through a third-party check printer, like those that advertise in the Sunday paper. The checks are just as good and a few dollars cheaper.

• Keep your receipts! Keep them until you see the transactions on your statement, at least, then use them to light the fireplace. It's a big pain in the butt digging through all those scraps of paper, but failing to get credit for a deposit is even worse. Banks make mistakes, too, and though they can dig through days of paperwork to find the error, they're not real happy to do so. And they can't always find the problem, especially if your memory of the exact date is somewhat hazy. If you get in the habit of keeping your receipts, even wadded up in a shoe box under the bed, I guarantee you that you'll avoid a major headache at some time in the future.

This advice is doubly important if you bank in a grocery store. Up here in Minnesota (and in Colorado and elsewhere), many banks are opening branches in stores like Cub Foods, Rainbow Foods, and so on, pushing the convenience aspect of banking while you shop for groceries. This is fine as far as it goes, but these grocery store branches are where all of the mistakes seem to happen.

During my stint as a customer service rep, I'd say that easily two-thirds of all bank errors originated in these grocery store branches. There are always huge lines, crying children, drunks, and people in a big hurry, all packed into a space the size of a gas station rest room. Be warned: *always* check your receipt for accuracy before you move from your spot in front of the teller's window, and *keep* that receipt until you verify the accuracy of your statement.

- Don't check your balance over the phone, from a teller, or at the ATM. Whatever balance you're given will be correct, technically, but it won't list checks and charges that haven't cleared yet. The bank-by-phone service or teller won't, after all, be able to tell you what checks of yours are getting traded at the Federal Reserve (or are sitting in another teller's drawer) that day. Getting your balance from the bank in this manner is bound to screw you up and cost you hours of freedom. Wait until you get your statement, then reconcile it with your checkbook every month. All you have to do is turn your bank statement over, follow the directions, and *voila!* Unfortunately, the instructions aren't all that straightforward, at least not from my bank. Here's what to do:

  1) Verify the check numbers and amounts on your statement with the ones in your check register. Make a little check mark both in your register and on your statement for the checks that have cleared. Do the same thing with ATM withdrawals and any fees you may have incurred. Cross-check your deposits the same way.
  2) Look over the area of your check register you were working in. Are there any entries that haven't cleared

yet? Chances are, there will be. If the back of your statement has a preprinted form with spaces to write down debits (money coming out of your account), write these down in the spaces provided. Ditto with checks or ATM transactions you made after the date/number where your statement cuts off.

3) Write down any deposits you've made since the statement cut off and subtract your impending debits from this figure. Hopefully, it's still a positive number. Add this to the ending balance shown on your statement.

But what if your balance and the bank's are still way off? Because my grandma is a psychic, I can foretell that 80 percent of the time, the bank is going to say that you've got less money than your check register says. That's due to three reasons: first, your bank probably slipped you a few fees when you weren't looking. These will be listed on your statement. Second, you probably forgot to write down some ATM and/or debit card transactions. These will also be listed on your statement, conspicuous by the fact that you didn't make check marks by them. Third, you suck at math. Round your numbers like I tell you elsewhere in this chapter, and use a calculator.

• Nowadays some merchants are refusing to accept checks numbered under 1500 or 2000 or some arbitrary threshold. Apparently they think that if you have higher-numbered checks, it means you've had a checking account for a long time. If this is a problem for you, talk to your bank customer service rep (or their supervisor) about getting your next order of checks printed with higher numbers on them. Just make up some bullshit reason about how the current series of numbers messes with your bookkeeping and it's quite likely that they'll let you do it. Many banks could care less what serial number is on your checks, as they don't use check numbers for their own records anyway. Here in Minneapolis, the minimum-number racket is becoming pretty popular, so the last time I ordered checks, I had them start at 5201.

- Banks like to cock off about how safe your money is when they've got it in the money bin. Well, they don't really have a money bin like Uncle Scrooge, they've got a vault, and there's not a heckuva lot of money in there. If you're the sort of person who's actually got a lot of money, you may wish to think about the following in order to avoid a big-time screwing in the future:

> First, banks like to talk about how your money is guaranteed, or insured, by the federal government via the FDIC, which stands for something I was too lazy to look up. Just kidding—it stands for Federal Deposit Insurance Corporation. It's true that funds on deposit (the money you hand over to them in exchange for numbers on paper) are insured by the federal government for up to $100,000 per individual and $100,000 per couple. Thus, you and your spouse can keep up to $300,000 in one bank and have it totally insured: $100,000 in your account, $100,000 in your spouse's, and $100,000 in a joint account. Sounds pretty good, huh?

> Except that all the money you have in the bank above that amount *isn't insured at all.* If you're a multimillion-aire (in which case I've got some business schemes I'd like to talk to you about) or a small businessman who deals with large sums of money (like a building con-tractor), I recommend that you keep no more than $300,000 in any bank. This warning also applies to people who have an IRA (Individual Retirement Account) at a bank, except, obviously, you can't have more than one IRA at a time.

> Back when the FDIC plan was set up, $100,000 would buy a third-world country. Unfortunately, a buck won't go as far as it used to, so wages had to rise, and so on. Anyway, due to inflation in prices and wages, common working stiffs can now look forward to accumulating almost $200,000 in an IRA over 30 years (assuming 6 percent interest and the maximum $2,200 per-person

contribution). This makes the lack of FDIC coverage over $100,000 a very real problem, doesn't it.

Second, FDIC insurance works about as well as you'd expect a program designed and run by the federal government to work—that is to say, hardly at all. Think about it: they're certainly not holding $100,000 in Fort Knox for every $100,000 you and everyone else in the country has on deposit. As a matter of fact, current estimates put the amount on reserve at somewhere between five and ten cents on the dollar. Better than nothing, certainly, but in the event of a massive series of bank failures (like the Savings and Loan debacle of a few years ago), expect to wait in line for months to get your five or ten percent settlement. Makes a home safe sound better and better, doesn't it?

(Note to potential burglars: I don't have a home safe. I've invested all my royalty checks in cardboard, three hundred thousand tons of which are stored in my backyard, patrolled by rabid German Shepherds armed with machine guns. Come and get it.)

I find it rather depressing that we've just gone through several pages of recommendations and cautions about banks, all of which relate to situations where the bank is allegedly taking care of your money. Banks "take care of" your money like the Mafia "took care of" Jimmy Hoffa. In the next chapter, we'll examine the way they treat you when you want to hold on to some of their money for awhile.

CHAPTER 6

THE HOUSE NEVER LOSES

Undoubtedly the largest loan most people will ever take out is to buy their own home. There are a lot of advantages to home ownership in today's America, such as being able to write off the mortgage interest and (hopefully, but not necessarily) an appreciation of the price after you buy it.

There are also a few downsides: property taxes, liability insurance, repair and replacement of major appliances, and having to cut your own lawn. Still, your only other alternative is to throw money away by renting. Think about it—at the end of 30 years of paying rent, you have nothing. At the end of 30 years of making house payments, even on the worst possible terms, you still have a house that's worth a fair chunk of change.

The government likes people to own their own homes because it keeps building contractors off welfare. No, just kidding; there are many reasons why your home ownership benefits the government, not the least of which is that it's a lot easier for them to seize your assets for back taxes if you stay in one place. So they allow you to write off the interest you pay each year. This may fall by the wayside in the future as the deductibility of credit card interest did, but right now it's still a good deal . . . in a way.

I'm continually amazed at how people talk about what a great deal it is to write off mortgage interest on their federal income tax return. The problem, to me, is obvious: even if you get to write off ten grand on your taxes, you're only getting 20 or 30 percent of your money back. Wouldn't it be better to pay the damn thing off and not pay *any* interest?

I know, I know. Most people can't afford to just write out a check for the balance on their mortgage. And there might be times when doing so would be a bad move. If you're making 20 percent a year on your money in the stock market, for example, it doesn't make much sense to liquidate early just to pay off something that is costing you 7 percent a year. Or maybe those multithousands of dollars in write-offs are keeping you out of a higher tax bracket. In cases like these, the mortgage interest deduction is better than nothing, but I refuse to get excited about it.

Banks like people to own their own homes, too (at least in name—in reality, of course, the bank owns the home until the last penny is paid). Banks like writing mortgages because they're making a loan backed by (typically) at least 110 percent collateral, which will last for 30 years and end up returning *four times* the loaned amount. They've rigged the game so that there are very few ways they can lose. They'll usually make you set up an escrow account to make sure that insurance and property taxes get paid on time, and the bank also gains interest on *that* money as it sits there.

Most people who take out mortgages today end up getting 30-year mortgages because they think the payments will be easier on their budget. Short term they're correct, sort of. Long term, they're dead wrong.

Banks love to write 30-year mortgages because they represent a *huge* increase in interest income for them. They don't want their beloved customers to find out that by paying as little as $50 or $100 extra per month, they could pay off their mortgage in 15 years rather than 30. Think about it: with the exception of the $18,000 you prepaid (12 months x $100 x 15 years, or often about 18 months' worth of payments), all the money they receive for those extra 15 years is going to be free money, frosting on the cake. Now this will vary a little, depending on the amount financed, the interest rate, and so on, but the principle is firm. I'll show you how to figure out all of this stuff in just a second.

Because mortgages have such long terms, it really pays to haggle over fractions of a percent on the interest rate. Let's take a look at the difference between 8 and 9 percent on a 30-year loan for $100,000. The formula we'll use for calculating this is the following somewhat daunting equation (if you'd rather skip the astrophysics, just jump ahead a couple of pages 'til we get to the end):

$$\frac{i \times (1 + i)^n}{(1 + i)^n - 1}$$

Where i equals the periodic interest rate divided by 100. The periodic interest rate is the interest rate they tell you you're getting, divided by the number of times per year the interest is compounded. In installment loans, like car and home loans, compounding usually takes place monthly. So with an installment loan at 9 percent, i is equal to 9 divided by 12, divided by 100, or .0075.

n in this case is equal to the number of payments to be made, so for a 30-year loan, n equals 30 x 12, or 360.

If it's been awhile since ninth grade algebra, remember your order of operations: first do the math in parentheses, then do exponents (the little raised numbers that tell you how many times to multiply a number by itself), multiplication, division, addition, subtraction. Now that we know what we're dealing with, let's work the math:

9 percent	**8 percent**

$$\frac{.0075 \times (1 + .0075)^{360}}{(1 + .0075)360 - 1} \qquad \frac{.0067 \times (1 + .0067)^{360}}{(1 + .0067)360 - 1}$$

$$\frac{.0075 \times (1.0075)^{360}}{(1.0075)^{360} - 1} \qquad \frac{.0067 \times (1.0067)^{360}}{(1.0067)^{360} - 1}$$

$$\frac{.0075 \times 14.731}{14.731 - 1} \qquad \frac{.0067 \times 11.067}{11.067 - 1}$$

$$\frac{.1105}{13.731} \qquad \frac{.0741}{10.067}$$

$$.008 \qquad .007$$

Next, we multiply each of these figures by the amount you financed (say a nice, round number like $100,000) to find your estimated monthly payment:

$$100,000 \times .008 = 800 \qquad 100,000 \times .007 = 700$$

Finally, we multiply each amount by 360, or the number of payments you'll make over the term of the loan:

$$360 \times 800 = 288,000 \qquad 360 \times 700 = 252,000$$

So by getting a loan at 8 percent rather than 9, you're saving yourself $36,000 (after taxes!), or about a year and a half's work for the average person (actual income, not the pretax B.S. income everyone pretends they make).

Now let's see how much your monthly payment and the total amount you pay would differ if you got a 20-year mortgage instead of a 30. We'll compare both 8 and 9 percent, figuring a loan amount of $100,000.

9 percent	**8 percent**
$\dfrac{.0075 \times (1 + .0075)^{240}}{(1 + .0075)240 - 1}$	$\dfrac{.0067 \times (1 + .0067)^{240}}{(1 + .0067)240 - 1}$
$\dfrac{.0075 \times (1.0075)^{240}}{(1.0075)^{240} - 1}$	$\dfrac{.0067 \times (1.0067)^{240}}{(1.0067)^{240} - 1}$
$\dfrac{.0075 \times 6.009}{6.009 - 1}$	$\dfrac{.0067 \times 4.966}{4.966 - 1}$
$\dfrac{.0451}{5.009}$	$\dfrac{.0333}{3.966}$
.009	.008
$.009 \times 100,000 = 900$	$.008 \times 100,000 = 800$

So by getting a 20-year mortgage instead of a 30-year, your monthly payments would only go up about $100. Let's see how much you'd save in the long run:

$$900 \times 240 = 216,000 \qquad\qquad 800 \times 240 = 192,000$$

By adding a measly $100 each month to your mortgage payments, you'd save $72,000 (at 9 percent) or $60,000 (at 8 percent), all of which is pure profit for the bank. No wonder they don't want you to know your math!

Just for fun, let's figure out how much you'd have at the end of those last 10 years (30 year mortgage paid off in 20 leaves 10 years) if you put your monthly payment, say $800, in a series of CDs or in a money market fund. We'll assume a 6 percent return and a pathetic compounding frequency (yearly). The math gets a little hairy here, so I'll spare you the equations and apply a little "Tennessee windage" to get an approximate amount:

Year #	Amount Deposited	Amount Accrued
1	$9,600.00	$9,840.00
2	$9,600.00	$20,270.40
3	$9,600.00	$31,326.62
4	$9,600.00	$43,046.22
5	$9,600.00	$55,468.99
6	$9,600.00	$68,637.13
7	$9,600.00	$82,595.36
8	$9,600.00	$97,391.08
9	$9,600.00	$113,074.54
10	$9,600.00	$129,699.02

Just think—if you hadn't paid that $100 per month during the first 20 years, at the end of 30 years you'd have . . . a house. But by paying that extra money, at the end of 30 years you've got a house *plus* $130,000 in the bank. You could also say that you got a $100,000 house for $62,000, if we subtract the amount you have in savings from your total mortgage payments.

Of course, your house might cost much less. Most banks compound their CDs quarterly rather than yearly, which is a better deal for you. Maybe you'll even be able to find a bank that compounds monthly. You could probably also find a better rate than 6 percent. And if you put $2,000 of each year's $9,600 into a Roth IRA instead of into a CD, you'll earn the same interest as on a CD, but that interest will be tax-free. In the above example, that would mean that you're effectively earning maybe a third more on about 20 percent of the money, or about $8,000 more over the course of 10 years.

So what if you bought this book and you've already got a mortgage? Well, there are a couple of things you can do. First, you could refinance. As I write this, mortgage rates are lower than they have been in perhaps 10 years, and as a consequence, people are lining up to refinance.

If you're self-employed, however, you'll find that banks aren't all that eager to loan money to you, no matter how much collateral you have to put up. In that case, your only option is to write your monthly checks out for more than the amount on the payment coupon. Hey, just because you took out a 30-year mortgage doesn't mean you can't turn it into a 20-year plan. Just make sure that your mortgage doesn't have a clause assessing a penalty for paying it off early. If it does have such a clause, well, you'll know better next time, won't you?

You'll need to check with your bank or mortgage company to find out how to send in the extra money; some recommend writing out two checks, one for the normal amount and one marked "to be applied to principle" or something. Other banks automatically apply overpayments to the principle.

By the way; if you're thinking about buying a house, you're going to have to save up a down payment, typically 10 percent of the purchase price. What's the best way to do that?

The absolute worst way, obviously, is to keep the money in cash buried in the backyard. In addition to problems with mold, the money won't earn any interest and will actually lose value due to inflation.

Only marginally better is to put your money in a regular old savings or checking-with-interest account. You earn pathetic interest *and* you have to pay taxes on any interest income over $400.

A CD sounds like a good way to go because you get better interest, but you can't add money to a CD every two weeks. And there's still the problem with taxes on the interest.

Another way to go is to open up a Roth IRA at a bank and put in the maximum yearly amount. Not only do you gain the same interest as the bank offers on long-term CDs, but you can add to your account as often as you'd like. And with Roth IRAs, you never pay taxes on the interest you earn. This is only the best deal if you're a first-time home buyer, however. Under current legislation, first-time home buyers can withdraw up to $10,000 to apply to the purchase of their house without paying any penalties whatsoever.

Other places than banks, mostly stock brokerages, can open up a Roth IRA for you, too, and usually your rate of return will be higher. However, the growth rate on stock-based IRAs cannot be guaranteed, so you could find yourself losing money for months or years at a stretch. Personally, I like to draw a line between stuff I need to be super safe, like retirement accounts, and stuff I know I'm gambling with, like whatever money I throw at the stock market. The choice is yours, however.

The only problem with opening a Roth IRA for your first house is that current legislation says the account has to be open five years before you can withdraw your ten grand. Maybe you're better at long-range planning than me and my wife, but what we chose was a money market fund. Money market funds are generally peddled by brokerage houses and have the following advantages:

- They pay roughly the same interest as CDs.
- They're 98 percent as safe as CDs.
- They're completely liquid—you can pull your money out at any time without penalty.

Since we didn't want to wait five years to buy our house, and since we wanted our money to be 98 percent safe and 100 percent liquid, we signed up for a money market fund to accumulate cash for our down payment. Anyway, back to mortgages and so forth:

What if you need a house but don't want to take out a loan or can't qualify for one? You still have a few options:

1) You can find someone who's willing to let you "contract for deed." What this means is, Joe Homeowner agrees to let you make payments toward the purchase of his pad, but if you stop making payments, he gets the place back. This can be a really good option if you move in, then find that the house is full of radon or something. Caution: make Joe prove he owes the place free and clear before you make the first payment. If the bank owns the paper on the house, they'll take it from *you* if Joe doesn't make *his* payments. You'll have to go after Joe in court to try to get your money back, and good luck with that.

2) You could buy a HUD (Housing and Urban Development) home from the government. If you're handier with a hammer than I am, this can be a really great deal (HUD homes frequently require some repairs in order to meet local housing codes). Prices for houses on this sort of plan supposedly start at one dollar. Caution: do a thorough inspection of a HUD property before you sign any paperwork. If the place sits over a pond of toxic waste or an Indian burial ground, you'll be stuck with the legal hassles. After all, there must be *some* reason the original homeowner let it get taken over by the government.

3) You could contact your local city or county property tax assessor's office to find out about property seized for nonpayment of taxes. While I as a Libertarian don't like to encourage government theft of private property, you may not feel quite so strongly about the issue. Generally they'll let you take a property just for paying the back taxes due, maybe a couple thousand dollars' worth. As with a HUD home, however, you may have to bring any buildings up to code before you move in.

4) You can contact local banks to see whether they have any recent foreclosures up for sale. Strangely enough, banks often will take a lower price for seized collateral because they can always sue the borrower for any amount he still owes after the foreclosure sale goes through. Still, they're not dummies—you may not find the same bargain-basement prices as you would through HUD or the county.

5) Think about moving to a small town. Not only are the people friendlier but the crime rate's lower and real estate prices are in

the toilet. In my hometown of Garvin, Minnesota, it was still possible a couple of years ago to buy a two-bedroom house in good repair, plus major appliances and satellite dish, for $5,000. Think about *that* when property tax season rolls around—like, how about a $50 tax bill instead of one for $2,000? That's 195 hours (almost five weeks) of paid vacation per year, my friend. Also expect to enjoy huge cuts to your auto and homeowner's insurance premiums compared to living in a metro area.

CHAPTER 7

THE TAX MAN COMETH

I 've got a great deal for you: pay me a couple hundred dollars out of each paycheck, every week, and once a year I'll give you the money back without paying you any interest on it.

You'd think only a loon would go for a boneheaded deal like this . . . but millions of taxpayers take Uncle Sam up on this offer every year.

Every time one of my friends starts talking about what a great tax refund check they got from "Big Unc," I start ranting at them.

"You idiot!" I scream. "Don't you realize you lose 3 or 4 percent on your money by having all those taxes taken out? You could put that cash in a money market account instead and make money on those tax dollars!"

Well, it seems like hardly anyone ever listens. They're used to my frequent outbursts, and they know that once they dose me with enough beer I'll settle down and go to sleep.

But my point is a valid one: people who get money back from the government every year are having *way* too much money deducted from their paychecks. By talking to the human resources department at work and increasing the number of deductions on your W-4 form, you will get bigger paychecks every week.

Of course, you still have to pay your taxes. No one I've heard of has found a way of dodging those. Well, rich guys like Bill Gates can afford to hire shysters to trim the fat out of their tax bills, but people like you and me still have to go down to H&R Block.

But just because you have to pay your taxes doesn't mean you can't get some benefit out of the money that is nominally yours. Take a look at your last couple years' tax returns. If you figure you're going to earn about the same amount this year, then you know, roughly, how much you're going to have to pay in state and federal taxes.

Now the chances are good that you're not going to qualify for exemption from withholdings; that is, the tax man is going to take *some* of your paycheck. The purpose of maximizing your deductions is to have him take out as little as possible. Anyway, once you've decreased the withholding bite as much as possible, take a look at your pay stub to see how much you still got nicked.

If you're one of those folks who works a salaried job, then your paychecks are probably about the same from pay period to pay period. Assuming you get paid every two weeks (more and more common in these grim times), then you can multiply the federal taxes withheld by 26 (for the number of pay periods in a year, right?) to get the amount which will be withheld over the course of a year. Now subtract that figure from the amount you paid in federal taxes last year and you'll get a rough figure for what you have to save up to pay your taxes come April 15 in addition to what they've already withheld. Divide that by 26 and you'll know how much out of each paycheck to put in savings to cover the amount. Do the same for state taxes.

Alright, alright, here's an example:

Milo Mindbender paid $4,500 in federal taxes last year and $450 in state taxes. After reducing the bite withheld from him from each paycheck, Milo notices that $150 out of each biweekly paycheck goes to the feds and $12 goes to the state. He multiplies each of these by 26, getting an approximate yearly withholding of $3,900 for federal and $312 for state taxes. He subtracts those figures from the taxes he paid last year, which tells him he's probably going to have to contribute an additional $600 to the feds and $138 to the state. Thus, his April 15 out-of-pocket tax liability is going to be $738. He divides that by 26 to see how much out of each paycheck he's going to tuck in the bank. Turns out it's about $28.38. He'll put away $30 each time he gets paid just to err on the safe side.

How much is Milo going to make in interest off of Uncle Sam? Well, it's a real bitch of an equation, because we're dealing with fractions of a year, but we can approximate. At the end of the year, he's got $780 in the bank, some of which has been there 11.5 months and some of which has been there only a couple of weeks. We'll be off by a little bit if we just split the saved amount in half and multiply it by the rate of interest, but what the heck, it's only a couple of cents. If Milo's getting 4.5 percent on his money (a fair guess at the time this book is written), he'll end up making an extra $17.55 or so (plus compounding). Not a whole lot, but equal to about two hours of his real wage.

You may not think 17 bucks is enough to bother with, but c'mon; if you saw $17 lying on the sidewalk, you'd pick it up. Besides, when interest rates go up again we could see banks offering savings accounts at 8 or 9 percent, just like we saw in the 1970s. That brings Milo's interest income up to maybe $65. Also, if Milo had to save more than $30 per paycheck, he'd get more interest earnings. At the time this is being written, you don't have to pay federal income tax on interest income up to $400, so I hasten to add that Milo's windfall is also *tax free*.

Caveat: this special savings account is not for buying a boat, fixing the truck, or paying off other bills. This is only for taxes. If you don't have the self-discipline to pay money into this account, week after week, no matter what, and not touch it, you're going to end up in a heap of trouble when Big Unc comes around with his hand out. Hey, there's no shame in it—some people need the interest-free enforced savings program that Uncle Sam runs. If you're one of them, go ahead and keep doing things the way you've been doing them. Just don't brag about your big tax refund to me.

Another way to cut your federal tax is by dumping money into an IRA or 401(k) plan. The standard IRA allows you to put pretax dollars into an account, provided you don't withdraw it until you reach a certain age. That is, you get to write off IRA contributions on your federal income tax. When you take it out you get socked for taxes, but if you're retired at this time, your income will be much less, so hopefully you'll be taxed at a lesser rate.

But starting in January 1998, Congress actually did something that helped the people who pay their salaries—they came up with a few new IRA plans. Now, we're not going to get into the benefits and drawbacks of each, because this book isn't really about that. There are plenty of good books on the market (some of which are listed in the bibliography) written by people who like to wear suits and ties that expound on figuring out which IRA is best for you. I just want to take a second to tell you a little more about the Roth IRA.

The Roth IRA is kind of like a traditional IRA turned upside-down. Instead of investing pretax dollars, you invest regular money, but once it's in there, you (according to current law) *never pay taxes on it again*. Not when you get your interest statement, not when you pull it out, never. Depending on your tax bracket, this can be the equivalent of adding 28 percent or more to the rate the bank or whoever says you're getting.

Now obviously it doesn't make much sense to dump $2,000 a year into an IRA that pays 6 percent when you're paying 18 percent, compounded monthly, on credit card bills unless you're saving more in tax write-offs than you're paying in credit card interest and fees. For the average person, that might be $660 a year or so (I'm assuming a 28 percent tax rate). But what about a 401(k)?

A 401(k) is a lot like an IRA, but your employer gets to kick in some bucks, too. Like an IRA, all contributions are tax-deductible, and all interest income is tax-deferred until you cash out around retirement.

Some employers match all of your 401(k) contributions up to a certain amount each year. Some match only a certain percentage. But if you work for an employer who matches every dollar you put in, up to $2,000 or so, you're getting an effective return of over 100 percent on your money (your $2,000 plus your employer's $2,000 plus whatever interest you make) *plus* you get to write off the contributions on your taxes. If you haven't taken the time to check up on the plan your employer offers because you don't think you can afford to contribute, I'm here to say that you might want to rethink that belief. But back to taxes . . .

There are other ways of decreasing your tax burden, of course. If you live in an area that borders another state, you've probably been taking advantage of the loopholes in both states. I live in Minnesota, for example, which doesn't tax things people need to live, like groceries and clothing, but which does have a fairly high state income tax. It also taxes the bejeezus out of things people need to forget about their crappy lives, like cigarettes and alcohol. People who live in the Dakotas, Iowa, and Wisconsin often cross the border to shop in Minnesota when they need to get groceries so they don't pay sales tax on them. Of course, Minnesotans will drive to Iowa or a local Indian reservation to get discount cigarettes and beer, so it works both ways.

The point is, if you live within 15 or 20 miles of a border, you can often find a way to make the other state's tax laws work for you, and not just when it comes to smuggling firecrackers. Hey, take a trip once a month and buy six cases of beer at a pop—maybe you'll get a volume discount, too. If your border state is one that has a deposit on cans and bottles, bring along your locally bought beverage containers to make 5 or 10 cents on each one. Again, most border-dwellers have probably figured this out for themselves, but I'm just tryin' to be helpful, folks.

Another way to dodge sales tax is to order high-priced items that you would buy anyway through the mail. I collect rare coins, for example, and I often place several-hundred-dollar orders to dealers in other states. This costs me three bucks in shipping, but I'd be paying $13 in sales tax (figuring a $200 order) if I bought them locally, so it's worth it for me to wait a week to get my coins and save $10 in the process.

Do the comparisons yourself, weighing the cost of shipping against the sales tax you'd have to pay. If you were buying gourmet firewood from Michigan, for example, I doubt you'd save any money over the gourmet firewood grown in your state, because the shipping cost would be a killer. Then again, if you're rich and/or stupid enough to be buying something as goofy as gourmet firewood, maybe you don't care.

If you take your taxes in to H&R Block or another accounting firm, don't forget that you can write off the cost of preparing that year's taxes on the next year's return. You may be able to come up with some other deductions, too; if you do anything remotely home-businesslike, maybe by doing woodworking or artsy-craftsy stuff on the side, you should start thinking about related expenses that you can write off on your taxes. Any long-distance calls? Any recent purchases of equipment? Any time spent driving around, picking up materials and supplies? These are all tax-deductible, and they'll help take a chunk out of your annual tax bite.

As a writer, I get to deduct all kinds of stuff: postage, phone bills, computer purchase and repair, mileage, college courses relating to writing, and so on. In 1997 I knocked $700 off my taxes without hardly trying.

You can save money on your property taxes simply by living somewhere cheap. Sounds obvious, I know, but you'd be amazed by the number of people who don't feel they've made it until they live in a suburb where they have to pay twice as much for a normal house as any sane person would.

I'm not saying you need to live in a ghetto. Randomly urinating winos can ruin your shrubbery, and while thundering airplanes and screeching sirens can provide you with that All-American Urban Experience, I can understand how you might eventually want some-one else to have the benefit of that experience for awhile. If you've got the stomach to deal with the blandness of the suburbs, by all means, flee.

But there are suburbs and then there are suburbs. Some of the ritzier ones won't let you put up lawn signs or park on the street. They wouldn't want people getting the wrong impression, you know—that anyone who lives there actually works for a living.

Two suburbs of St. Paul, Minnesota, Woodbury and Oakdale, lie just across the interstate from each other. Same bitterly cold climate, same constant whoosh of the freeway, same distance to downtown, but Woodbury's houses tend to be half again as expensive as Oakdale's. For my money, I'd take a house in Oakdale if I had to choose one of them, because not only am I going to be getting reamed less on the mortgage, my taxes are going to be a lot lower.

Again, I may not be telling you anything new, but it seems to me that an awful lot of people define *who* they are by *where* they live. People like this are wasting their money—an awful lot of it.

These ritzy suburb dwellers may defend their choice by saying that their house will appreciate in value faster than one across the interstate. They may be right, but I'd say they've been listening to the real estate agent a little too long. The reason housing prices are so ridiculous nowadays is because Baby Boomers came of age, and every damn one of them wanted a house. That sent the housing market through the roof, but what do you think is going to happen when these same Boomers hit retirement age and start checking in to retirement high-rises? Crash!

And what happens if your area loses an important industry, like when Detroit lost the auto industry? Crash! Some areas in Michigan have seen *blocks* of abandoned houses simply because people left the area to find work.

Right. We're supposed to be talking about taxes. But just one final point about houses—never buy a house expecting to sell it in 5, 10, or 20 years and make a bundle of money. Buy a house because you're sick of paying rent, or because you want more room for the kids, or because you want to have a garden. Sure, I think you could make a very good case that real estate prices will tend to go up *on average, in the long run*. After all, they're not making any more land (I'm not talking about garbage islands in New York Harbor). But that doesn't mean that your house will automatically go up in value. It might not for 50 years. Maybe never. Still, once you get the sucker paid off, owning your own home can be pretty cheap, and whether its value goes up or down, it'll still be a nice addition to your net worth.

CHAPTER 8

YOU BET YOUR LIFE

When you take out an insurance policy, what you're really doing is placing a bet. You're betting that you'll die, or become disabled, or have your house burn down, or whatever, and they're betting that you won't. Like casinos, insurance companies don't like it when you cheat. No fair being sneaky and burning your own house down or ramming your car into a tree because you want to cash out.

Also like casinos, insurance companies are not in the habit of losing. They know they'll have to pay a claim here and there, but they know they've got the statistical edge. Insurance companies charge you enough for each premium so that their bet is covered *and* they make some money.

It shouldn't be any surprise, then, that there are some bets you should take and some you should avoid. And just like in Vegas, you can get better odds by going across the street to another house.

Car insurance is a wager that almost everyone places, thanks to state law, and all companies look at the same things when setting odds: the driver's age, sex, marital status, number of accidents and/or tickets in the past three (sometimes five) years, and the make and model of their vehicle. It may come as some surprise, though, that insurance rates vary wildly from company to company.

How two companies can look at the same variables and come up with two different figures, hundreds of dollars apart, is beyond me.

The obvious answer, of course, is that one of them is trying to rip you off in a major way, but my lawyer tells me this is never the case. Doubtless it's a cosmic mystery.

In any case, *somebody's* paying those inflated premiums. Maybe it's you. If you have your auto insurance with, say, American Family Insurance because they insure your house, or because dad always went with American Family, it's time to shop around. Cruise the Yellow Pages, check out the Internet, or call those agentless companies like GEICO. It's definitely worth a couple hours of your life to do some comparison shopping.

The results you find may make you want to go down to your current agent's office and punch him in the nose, an action which my lawyer assures me I don't want to encourage you to perform. Just take your business elsewhere, and tell all your friends about the great new casino you found.

Much of the following information comes from a book called *Die Broke* by Stephen M. Pollan (and collaborator Mark Levine), who is an actual investment counselor in New York. His book has a lot of useful tips in it (though I disagree with his affection for debit cards), and he's more knowledgeable about fancy investment plans than I am. He's probably better in bed than I am, too—anything to keep his publisher's lawyers off my doorstep.

Life insurance is something that most people get around to buying sooner or later. Properly, it should be called "life span insurance," as in this case, the bet is not whether you'll die but when.

I really can't see a point to buying life insurance before you have a family to support. If you're a single person, the most you really need is a few grand to make sure you get planted, and if you want the Super Saver plan, you can get cremated or thrown off the side of a ship. I myself plan to be shot into deep space inside a talking casket.

If you do have a family, you have two insurance choices: term and whole life. Term insurance pays out a fixed amount when you die; whole life is kind of like a weird investment plan that lets you do all sorts of fancy things like borrow against the amount you've built up in the policy. A lot of agents like to push whole life policies, citing the fact that your money is invested for you, but whole life policies have been mangy dogs as far as returns on investment go. Insurance agents push whole life policies because they make a helluva lot more money on them, that's all. You want term, and no frills to go along with it.

Stay away from multiple-payoff policies, which specify that you have to die in an airplane crash, on a weekend, and so forth. Insurance companies offer these policies because they understand statistics better than you or I could ever hope to. The only people who ever cash in on these types of policies are insurance agents.

Another thing to avoid is the tendency to insure yourself for millions of dollars. Think about it—when you die, how long will it take your family to get back on their feet? What kind of other resources will they have to draw upon? Do you have other life insurance or a pension at work? Do you have an IRA or 401(k) which they'll be able to access when you die? The most insurance the average person really needs is enough to replace his salary for a couple of years, nothing more. That means a policy for perhaps $100,000 or so.

Remember, the odds are that you'll end up living until you're about 80, in which case you'll have cashed in on all of your investments and you'll (hopefully) be getting Social Security to boot. If you die at 80 and your spouse gets a $10,000,000 insurance settlement, she'll live well for a few years, but when she dies the government will get about half of what's left. Why pay extra on those premiums for the next few decades just to give half of it to the government?

Sit down and take a hard look at how much coverage your family will really need, then start shopping for the best rate.

As far as other types of insurance go, remember that location does make a difference. If you're thinking about moving from the Big City to the suburbs or a rural area, insurance savings are one thing you should consider.

Remember too that anything you've got a loan on, you're paying insurance on. By paying off a car loan or mortgage early, you're not only saving yourself interest charges but you're giving yourself the option to drop and/or reduce your insurance coverage. When I had a loan on my truck, I paid it off early, thus allowing me to save $30 per month on insurance costs. That's $360 per year, or almost a full week of work.

If you're not going to be able to pay that loan off for awhile, check with your bank to see how large a deductible they'll let you take. It is always, always, always worth it to have the highest deductible they'll allow, unless of course you have a habit of getting into accidents or starting grease fires on the stove. Once you take out a deductible, sock away those extra savings. Things happen, and you'll feel better about writing a $500 check if you know that it's money you would have ordinarily spent on your premiums anyway.

Should you be honest with your insurance company? Well, sort of. I'm sure it's probably against the law to lie to your insurance company, so I certainly am not going to recommend that you do so. However, if insurance goons ever come to your door, you probably could make a decent case that you "forgot" some stuff or didn't think about mentioning certain factors because you didn't know they were interested in your history of hit-and-run accidents. Here are some things you should keep in mind:

When you're checking out insurance rates on a car you recently purchased, you'll be asked how many tickets you've racked up in the past few years. The insurance company will pull a copy of your driving record, and it's a cinch that they'll catch you lying about any violations that occurred in the state you live in. Any tickets you get in *another* state, however, will be your little secret.

You see, insurance companies aren't going to go to all of the time and expense of pulling records from all of the 50 states. They figure that if you've gotten any tickets, the odds are good that you got them in your own state. Well, maybe or maybe not, depending on how much you travel.

Another thing: while insurance companies will certainly pull a copy of your driving record when you first take out a policy, the chances are very good that they'll never check your record again *as long as you don't change your coverage in any way*. If you happen to get a DWI, it may be a lot cheaper for you to keep paying for full coverage, even when you've paid your car off, than to risk them pulling a new copy of your driving record.

Of course if you live in a small town, all bets are off. The chances are good that your insurance agent reads the paper and will see your name in the "court report" section. But if you live in a big city, well, anonymity has its benefits.

When I signed up for coverage with GEICO, the customer service rep asked me if I always wore my seat belt. "Of course," I lied, and then asked him, "Does anybody ever say 'no' to that question?" Apparently some people do, and you can bet they pay higher rates for their honesty.

Check with your insurance agent to see what other options they can come up with as far as cutting your bill is concerned. Some companies give discounts for burglar and car alarms, some charge extra for keeping a live bear in your backyard. Many companies give discounts for multiple cars they insure or if you have both your homeowner's and auto coverage with them. Don't go so hog-wild over these discounts that you forget to shop around, however. The thing to always keep in mind about insurance is that it's just a product, like anything else, and you can usually buy it cheaper or with less frills somewhere else.

CHAPTER 9

YOUR UTILITY BILLS

I really wish I could've thought of a snappy title for this chapter, but let's face it: there's nothing real exciting about utility bills. You pay 'em as they come in. The best way to minimize your utility bills, of course, is not to have any. Call the power, gas, cable, and phone companies and tell 'em you're not going to be held in thrall to them any longer.

But hey, I'm not an ogre. I understand that taking this course might save you a few hundred bucks a month but might cost you a marriage. Besides, look at what happened to Ted Kaczynski.

Let's face it: you may bitch about the size of your electric bill, but it *is* nice to have lights and refrigeration. What we need to do is get your utility bills down to the lowest possible levels. Since each of your utility services is different, we'll attack them once at a time:

- The phone company sure does like to push extra "services." You can get Caller ID, Voice Messaging, Three-way Calling, Call Waiting, Speed Dialing, and all sorts of other junk. Now while I'm sure you could give me a good reason as to why, in some strange set of circumstances, you might need one of these services, the chances are good that 95 percent of the time you won't.

  Instead of paying $6.95 (plus tax) per month (or $83.40 per

year) for Voice Messaging, why not just buy an answering machine? You can get a really fancy answering machine for $83, and it'll likely last you for years. My answering machine cost $3 at a garage sale, and it works just fine. Annual savings: maybe $30–40 the first year, $83.40 annually as long as your machine lasts.

As to the rest of the stuff, the Call Waiting, the Caller ID, the Speed Dialing, and the rest of it, well, you don't need it. You could end up paying $200 a year or more for all these extra services. Why not pocket that money instead? Don't worry about missing messages when you cancel Call Waiting; it's my experience that getting a busy signal makes the caller feel *compelled* to call back. And even though you may be currently paying for speed dialing, be honest: can you really remember whose numbers you've programmed? Do you update the numbers in storage when your friends and relatives move? Or have you lost the instructions months ago? What you need is Touch-tone service for about a buck. That's the only option anyone really needs.

There's another thing that the phone company likes to charge you for. It's called Line Backer, and it's basically an insurance policy. This policy supposedly ensures that should you lose phone service and the problem is inside your house, you don't have to pay for any repairs. Well, this coverage costs about $2 a month, and over the past decade or so I've saved about $500 by declining it. And I've never had a problem with phone service that I've had to pay for. I recommend that you avoid this policy.

The phone company also wants you to pay an extra buck or two per month for an unlisted or nonpublished number. Actually having to pay for *not* having a service performed (being listed in the directory) is kind of strange, but that's the way it is. If you value your privacy, though, or if you're ducking bill collectors, there's a free alternative to being unlisted: sign up for your phone service under an assumed name or under your middle name instead of your first. This approach has the added benefit of letting friends and relatives look you up in the directory (assuming, that is, that you've told them the name you're listed under) while being able to screen telemarketers who are cold-calling.

- Boy, there sure are a lot of long-distance companies out there. There's the big three—AT&T, Sprint, and MCI-WorldCom—then there's a bunch of smaller companies that no one's ever heard of. And, curiously enough, they *all* have the cheapest rates (at least according to their commercials). Which one should you pick?

  Pick the cheapest one. There is virtually no difference between the service offered by the various long-distance companies, so the only real factor to keep in mind is cost. Back when the rate wars were hot and heavy, I used to switch long-distance companies every couple of months. A telemarketer would give me a call and make a pitch about their current specials. I'd talk him into throwing in a check for $50 and frequent-flyer miles and we'd call it a done deal.

  Unfortunately, those days are probably long gone (at least until the local phone service industry becomes deregulated), because the companies wised up to the fact that I and other canny consumers were playing them, like chumps, against each other and laughing all the way to the bank. Still, you might get a call from a company offering a special. Be sure to give it a good listen, and keep an ear perked for the "catch." If you can't find one, feel free to switch.

- I'm continually amazed that television cable companies still exist. Up here in Minneapolis, people with rabbit ears on their TVs can get clear reception of ABC, CBS, NBC, Fox, PBS, UPN, and assorted religious and home-shopping channels. But for only $50 a month ($600 a year), the cable companies are happy to provide you with the channels you'd get anyway, plus a bunch of fairly useless ones. The movie channels, like HBO and Cinemax, are an extra $10 or $15 a month. Face it: if you live in the Big City, you really *don't* need cable, or, for that matter, a satellite dish. You're looking at a week and a half, at hard labor, each year for stuff you probably don't watch that much anyway.

  If you live in the sticks, however, things are a little different. Maybe you only get one channel, and that one's snowy. I've found that cable rates are generally cheaper in small towns, maybe 15 or 20 bucks a month. You're on your own, here—I'm not going to stand between you and your TV. Basic cable is OK; anything else is probably a waste of money. Really, how many times can you watch *Mannequin II* on Cinemax without vomiting? Rent the thing for a couple of bucks if you like it so much, and you can watch it over and over for 24 hours.

- You probably don't have much choice about where you get your electricity or gas service, but you do have a choice about which is the more cost-effective for you. Personally, I live in an apartment because my fancy-free lifestyle as a Big Time Author doesn't include time for cutting the lawn every week. As a consequence, my electric and gas bills are only about $8 a month each.

   But if you're a homeowner (or a home renter), you may be looking at a couple of hundred a month. You've got more space, more stuff, and hence use more energy. Well, there are ways to save on gas and electricity that you may not have thought of, and hey, a buck saved is a buck you don't have to earn.

1) Up here in Minnesota, our power company is primarily NSP (not counting the numerous rural electric co-ops). Homeowners and renters serviced by NSP can have a company rep come out to their house and perform a sort of energy-efficiency study, pointing out places where less energy could be used. Power companies have got to be the only businesses in existence that keep trying to sell you less of their product. Anyway, it's free, so why not take advantage of it? You could end up with some options that could pay for themselves within a year.

2) In the winter, if you have a winter, put that shrinky plastic stuff up over your windows. Windows are huge heat-losers, especially older windows, and you'll be saving money *plus* making your pad warmer. The cost to treat a large apartment is 10 bucks or so; a house might cost double that, but you'll be amazed at the difference it makes.

3) Always keep your refrigerator full of *something*, and sweep the dust off the black coils on the back of it every couple of months. If you generally don't have much in your fridge, you're better off filling gallon jugs full of tap water and leaving them inside it. You see, water holds heat (in this case, lack of heat) better than air does, and your refrigerator won't have to work as hard to pump the heat out. The black coils on the back of the fridge are where all of the heat from inside your refrigerator ends up. Dust, cat hair, and other junk keeps them from radiating heat as efficiently, and so your fridge has to "run" more frequently.

4) Turn down the heat in your house when you leave for work and/or go to bed, then back up when you're home and awake. This is an old trick that you might remember from the energy crisis of the 1970s, but it is one which can save you plenty of heating oil, gas, or electricity during chilly weather. The less heat that is in your house, the less is going to leak out.

5) During the summer, and for those of you in hot climates, air conditioning can be a real money drainer. It seems like most people like to keep their houses at a constant 68 or 70 degrees year-round. But in addition to being unhealthy, this approach is expensive. Instead, open all of the windows in the house at night when it's cool out, then close them up first thing in the morning and pull the shades down. Your house will stay pretty comfortable all day, and you'll be saving quite a bit of energy. If you must have air conditioning, try to cool as small a space as possible—there's no point in cooling rooms you rarely enter, like the guest bedroom, so keep those doors shut!

6) Turn out the lights when you leave the room. No shit, Sherlock—really? Really. I know it seems ridiculous to even mention this tip, but if you start paying attention to lights that get left on, you might be surprised at how frequently it happens.

7) Rather than running the dryer constantly, why not take a tip from mom and dad and put up a clothesline? Weather permitting, of course. It's tough to lose on this one; your clothes will smell good without the benefit of artificial fabric softeners (unless you run a hog farm), you'll be out in the sunshine, and you'll be saving a few bucks. In the winter, hang them up on one of those collapsible wooden drying racks.

• Unless you live in the country and have your own well, chances are you'll be paying a water bill. To cut down on your water consumption, you could install water-saver shower heads or throw the whole family in the tub at once, but in my experience these money-saving attempts lose a lot in the way of comfort.

One thing you can do to cut your water bill is to put stuff in your toilet tank. Most American toilets use more water to flush than they actually need, so you can fill some of the space in the tank with bricks or full bottles of water. Each time the tank refills (maybe five times a day, per person), you'll be saving a half a gallon or a gallon.

Another way to save water is to replace the washers in leaky faucets. This tip is probably no big revelation to you, as every home-handyman columnist brings it up. But let me back up their advice. If you can spend 30 cents for a washer that will trim 10 bucks a month off your water bill, isn't it worth it?

And while we're saving water, what about that lawn? Is it worth $20 a month or so in water for you to have an American Showpiece lawn, or can you deal with some brown spots here and there? If you live in a ritzy suburb, you may find your neighbors will make up your mind for you, but if you live in a trailer park, chances are your neighbors could care less. Just remember—the more you water it, the more you have to mow it.

• Remember that, generally, gas appliances are cheaper than electric ones. That's something to keep in mind when picking up a new dryer. Your gas and/or electric company may also offer rebates for buying energy-efficient appliances. You'll no doubt have to do some math on this one, weighing a possibly higher initial price for the appliance against the rebate and the monthly savings. Generally speaking, appliance stores are pretty forthcoming about this information, but always check with your utility company for the opinion of someone who doesn't work on commission.

CHAPTER 10

LET'S GET TO WORK

B y this point in the book, you've no doubt found a bunch of ways that you can save money (and therefore hours of your life). That's good enough as it goes, but I still haven't mentioned the system you'll use to get rid of the debt you're carrying around. It's pretty simple, actually, and it's the one I used myself.

I should mention that time is of the essence. Getting yourself out of debt is a process you can't afford to put off. Consider the interest charges you'll be paying, maybe the full-coverage insurance on a vehicle, and then consider the interest you're *losing* by not investing the money you're putting toward debt. Think it's insignificant? Think again.

Consider the case of this Roth IRA I keep cocking off about. Short term, sure, you're only losing maybe 10 bucks a month. But long term, hoo boy. For the sake of argument, let's say you chose to open a Roth IRA the day you turned 35, then cash it in on your 65th birthday. We'll say you made the maximum contribution each year, which is $2,000 at the time of this writing. We'll also say that you earned 6 percent APR for those 30 years (which is reasonable as I write this but is undoubtedly low as an average). To make the calculations easier, we'll say that you put in each year's contribution on your birthday. Let's look at the numbers:

Year	Interest Earned	Year-end Total
01	$132.00	$2,332.00
02	$271.92	$4,803.92
03	$420.23	$7,424.15
04	$577.44	$10,201.60
05	$744.09	$13,145.70
06	$920.74	$16,266.44
07	$1,107.98	$19,574.42
08	$1,306.46	$23,080.89
09	$1,516.85	$26,797.74
10	$1,739.86	$30,737.61
11	$1,976.25	$34,913.87
12	$2,226.83	$39,340.70
13	$2,492.44	$44,033.14
14	$2,773.98	$49,007.13
15	$3,072.42	$54,279.56
16	$3,388.77	$59,868.33
17	$3,724.10	$65,792.43
18	$4,079.54	$72,071.98
19	$4,456.31	$78,728.30
20	$4,855.69	$85,783.99
21	$5,279.03	$93,263.03
22	$5,727.78	$101,190.82
23	$6,203.44	$109,594.27
24	$6,707.65	$118,501.93
25	$7,242.11	$127,944.04
26	$7,808.64	$137,952.68
27	$8,409.16	$148,561.85
28	$9,045.71	$159,807.56
29	$9,720.45	$171,728.01
30	$10,435.68	$184,363.69
31	$11,193.82	$197,757.51

I included the 31st year because that shows how much tax-free interest income you're losing, really. Assuming you're going to need to take the money out at 65 and you're not yet 35, every month you delay costs you about $1,000 *or more* in lost future *tax-free* income.

Remember, we're taking care to guess on the low side here. Some stock IRAs pay a lot more than 6 percent, on average. No matter when you start your savings plan, you're going to go through the lean years of $100 and $200 yearly interest earnings. But the earlier you start, and the longer you keep from breaking into that savings plan, the more fat years of $12,000 in interest *and more* you'll get. So let's get to it.

First of all, I've said it before and I'm saying it again: there's no point in having $10,000 in savings or CDs or whatever at 5 percent if all of your debts are costing you 10 percent per year. You're also losing a couple more percent due to inflation, since the good ol' U.S. of A. no longer has gold-backed currency. If you're lucky enough to have a nest egg and you're not making anywhere near the sort of interest that you're paying, cash it in and get rid of those debts, then start a new savings program.

But what if you have nothing in savings, or maybe a thousand bucks or so? Then you have to do it the hard way, like I did. Don't bother starting a nest egg; it's tough to beat the rates you're paying now. The only exception to that statement is if you have a 401(k) at work where your employer matches your contributions at a higher rate than, say, $20 to your $100. That kind of return beats the worst credit card interest, even if you can't get your hands on the money right away. Here's what you need to do:

- Start by declaring your credit cards off-limits. At Consumer Credit Counseling, they cut them up, but I'm with-it enough to know that sometimes a bona fide emergency will come up, or sometimes you'll need to rent a car or whatever. If you don't think you have the willpower to stop buying stuff on credit, you might consider cutting up all your credit cards but one, or freezing them at the bottom of one of those old-fashioned aluminum ice-cube trays, or stashing the whole wad up in the closet underneath that tacky ceramic log lamp you got from Aunt Edna when you got married. That way you won't have the damn things with you, and you'll really have to go to some effort to get at them to charge something. Treat your credit cards like a loaded handgun and you'll be OK.

Again, there's an exception. If you can get no-fee checks from your credit card company, you can make a few bucks a month at their expense in the way I outlined a few chapters ago. Do the same thing with stuff you'd normally buy for the house, or for gas, if you have the willpower not to spend the cash on booze and hookers.

Put away that ATM card, too. If you look through your checkbook, you'll probably see lots of ATM withdrawals for 10, 20, maybe 50 bucks, but I'd be surprised if you could remember what you spent the dough on. Nothing helps you spend money like an ATM or debit card, but it's our goal to make it harder for you to spend money.

• Having been a bill-payer for some time now, you probably have a pretty good idea of when your bills come due. First, sit down and figure out how much you reasonably need for spending money each week. Could be 20 bucks, could be 50, but pick a figure that will allow you some entertainment without being crazy about it. Subtract that figure from your weekly paycheck, or, if you get paid every two weeks, subtract double that amount from your biweekly check. That money is your fun money, and it's all you're going to get for awhile. If you're three days from payday and you're out of money, too bad. Nobody ever said this was going to be easy. What's left over is what you've got to work with.

Let's say it's $300 per week. Now sit down with a calendar and a pad of paper and write down every payday you have for the next six months or so. Under each date, write down what you need to pay out of that check. Juggle things around a little bit so the amount you're paying out of each check approaches but doesn't go over $300 per week. Don't forget to factor in things like groceries, gas, and so forth—things you don't actually get billed for but for which you have to pay anyway.

Not only will this method help you avoid late charges, but now you've got an organized way of looking at where your money's going. Once you get this schedule figured out, hang on to it. It's your map to financial freedom.

- If you find that you have extra money left over after meeting each bill's minimum payment, figure out which bills you should be throwing extra money at. It might be the smallest ones or the ones with the highest interest rates, or it might be bills that have added costs, like the full-coverage insurance on an auto loan. In my case it was my truck loan, which was costing me an extra $30 per month in full coverage (versus basic liability insurance). Put the extra money you have toward those bills, concentrating on one at a time.

- Once you have one bill paid off, pat yourself on the back and apply the money you had been sending to that creditor to the next bill on your priority list. That's literally all there is to it. Pretty soon you'll be able to be making double payments on your mortgage and cut the term by five or 10 years.

- Any unexpected money you receive, like inheritances and tax rebates, should go straight to bills. Okay, blow 10 percent of it on fun stuff if you have to just to get it out of your system, but promise me you'll pay off debt with the rest of it.

- If you're really in trouble with creditors (and I mean in collections with your credit cards shut off and/or foreclosure or repossession looming on the horizon), you could try for a settlement. Reaching a settlement means that you pay, say, 80 percent of your VISA bill in one chunk and the card issuer stops bugging you for the rest of the money. The amount you owe will still be listed on your credit report, but the lender will never again bug you about paying the remaining amount.

  Warning: this *will* affect your credit rating. How badly? Not very, actually. If you've gotten a couple of bills sent to collection agencies, or if Happy Harvey's Discount Cars is looking to repo your jalopy, your credit is pretty bad already. Paying the entire amount you owe won't significantly improve it, so you may as well go for a settlement.

  If at some time in the future you apply for another loan, the banker may want you to pay the amount you still owe, even if it's at another bank or with a credit card company. (Bankers know that they might get stuck with your next unpaid balance, so they form kind of a "Silent Brotherhood" which helps ensure that past debts are taken care of before future ones are incurred.) Fine. Do so if you wish. Gotrocks VISA will be happy to take your money, and you've just gotten an interest-free loan from them for several years. Hopefully, your finances will be in better shape, too.

It sounds deceptively simple, but assuming you don't incur any new debt, you should find yourself in the clear in eight years or less, including your mortgage.

Eight years??? Hey, it could be less, maybe much less. If you don't have a brand-new mortgage on your back, you could be looking at a year or two. Even if you just started paying on a house, you're bound to get a raise some day, maybe get an inheritance, who knows? The important thing is that you'll feel a sense of accomplishment every time you get one of those bills paid off, *plus* you'll be investing your money at 18 percent interest, compounded monthly.

Think about it: if you're not *paying* that kind of interest by paying those credit card bills off, you're essentially earning that kind of return on your time and money. And eventually, that day *is* going to come when you can hold up your head and say that you don't owe a dime to anyone on the face of the earth. Not too many Americans can say that. Then it's time to start making interest work *for* you rather than against you.

CHAPTER 11

NOW WHAT?

Sooner or later, you'll find yourself out of debt—that is, if you're persistent. Now what?

Well, you could choose to only work part time while maintaining the same lifestyle you'd been in, using the rest of the time to sleep in the shade or horse around with hobbies. Maybe you find that you get more satisfaction out of another job that pays less than you currently make. Maybe you'd rather sit around the kitchen and write books. Maybe you'd like to retire in Mexico. After all, you'll only have a couple hundred dollars per month in unavoidable expenses, and a fry-dipping job at McDonalds could cover that.

While life as a bum does have its attractions, I personally find that it lacks a certain something in the meaning-of-life department. I suggest that you keep working in some manner and invest the extra money you've created for yourself.

What? Keep working? Yep, that's right. You've been paying interest to other people for years—now it's time for other people to pay it to you. Nothing beats the feeling of opening up a statement from your bank or stockbroker and seeing how your money grew in the past month. Instead of working hard to no real benefit, you're now getting a real benefit without working hard. And isn't that the American way?

You're also getting on in years; if you followed my plan for getting rid of debt, you probably haven't had much of an investment plan to speak of. You need to start making up for lost time to ensure that you're not going to be eating dog food in your "golden years."

There are some really great books available, some of which are listed in the recommended reading section after this chapter, which will walk you through picking your own investments. The authors of these weighty tomes cover the subject better than I ever could, what with their really impressive degrees from Harvard and all, and they put the information forward in an easy-to-understand manner.

Generally, though, there are only a couple of things to keep in mind:

- Invest for the long haul, not for a month or a year. Whether you put your money into a mutual fund or buy a few pounds of gold to bury in the backyard, you need to keep your cool and not get spooked by market fluctuations.

  On the other hand, don't hesitate to clean out the losers. If a stock you've picked is a dog, shoot it.

- The best time to buy anything is right after the market crashes. At the time I write this, gold is under $300 an ounce, which is a bargain-basement price. At the same time, the stock market is at an all-time high. Guess where I'm putting my money?

- Be careful to leave yourself enough money in a savings account or other highly liquid place to cover you during emergencies. You could have all of your money in the best mutual fund in the world, but if you're forced to cash in when its value is down, you're still getting screwed. I speak from experience—investments can and will blow up in your face if you don't leave yourself a minor hoard of cash to deal with the occasional problem.

How much? It depends on a few different factors—what your monthly expenses are, how likely you are to get fired or laid off, and so on. Since an author's income is highly variable, to say the least, I like to keep at least six months' income in the best savings account

I can find. The interest I receive is usually pathetic, but I'd hate to have to cash in my vast cardboard empire in order to cover some unexpected expense.

You should probably be keeping just enough money to cover your expenses in some sort of money market or checking with interest account. Keep the rest of your short-term, highly liquid emergency cash in a money market fund.

Say you figure that you want to have $10,000 fairly close at hand in case you lose your job. Well, according to the budget you worked out in the last chapter, you'll have a little more than $1,200 each month that you can play with without touching your fun money. Throw $1,000 of it into your mutual fund. The other $200 you can invest in the markets, put into an IRA, or save up for something you've been wanting for awhile, like a car or a computer. Heck, you could even take a *real* vacation if you save it up for a year.

Once you get your safety net set up, of course, you can start investing your $1,200 a month any way you choose. After all, you're not paying bills with it. Get the best combination of growth and safety that you feel comfortable with.

Here are a few assorted tips about growing your money:

- If you check out a calendar, you'll notice that twice a year you get five paychecks instead of four (if you get paid weekly) or you'll get three biweekly paychecks instead of two. Just as we did with bills, these "bonus" checks should go straight into your investments. Okay, you can blow 10 percent if you feel you must. But invest the rest. The same goes for income tax returns, inheritances, and other money that you stumble across.

- Diversify, diversify, diversify. Putting all your eggs in one basket is setting yourself up for a fall. You should certainly have an IRA, at least, plus a 401(k) or 403(b), if your employer offers them. The tax benefits of these plans are just too cool to ignore. Aside from that, you'll only want to put a certain percentage of your money into stocks, bonds, money market funds, gold, treasury bills, and so forth. If you're a young punk like me, you can afford to shoot for the higher return of a riskier mix, but if you've only got 10 years until retirement, you'll want to go for stability first, then return. See some of the books in the recommended reading section for an in-depth analysis on how to diversify your money.

- One of the cool things about stocks, which doesn't happen with any other investment but livestock, is that they reproduce themselves. My grandfather bought seven shares of Norwest stock back in the 1930s, and that stock has turned itself into over a thousand shares by now. (Of course, the stock could've turned into worthless paper by now too.)

  Most people today who don't work on Wall Street invest in stocks by way of mutual funds. Mutual funds are sort of like what you might end up with if you and 1,000 of your closest friends got together, pooled your money, then hired some fancy-pants broker to juggle the stocks, bonds, and money market funds you dumped your money into.

  Just like anything else, there are good mutual funds and crappy mutual funds, and finding the good ones may require you to do some homework. Stay away from funds that are "loaded" (meaning you get charged a fee when putting money in or taking it out), and stay away from new funds. What you want is a fund that has a long (10 years or so) track record of decent returns. Now, just because a fund has done well in the past is no guarantee that it'll do well in the future. On average, though, we pray that past performers will generally make good in the future.

- One of the cool things about precious metals, like gold and silver, is that they're always going to be worth something. A modern tycoon's paper empire may crumble into dust during a stock market crash, but gold holds its value and can always be traded for other stuff.

  But buyer beware—there are plenty of places out there that capitalize on peoples' almost instinctive desire for gold by peddling precious metals to the ignorant at inflated prices. Before you buy precious metals, you *must* do your research. Check the listing in the paper (called "spot" by those of us in the know) and see what price gold is trading at. Then keep that figure in mind when investing in precious metals. Some people will buy a 10 ounce bar of silver for $75 when silver is trading for $5 an ounce just because they are uninformed of what the spot price of silver is.

Go down to your local bookstore and buy a couple of coin magazines. Inside you should find a dozen ads for people who want to sell you gold at perhaps 5 percent over spot or less. The same advice goes for silver.

I should mention here that "spot" is the price for a 5,000-ounce bar straight from the refinery. If you want your gold in smaller bars or coins, you're going to need to pay what's called a "premium," or an added charge to have the gold minted into a more attractive form. Different bars and coins have different premiums; 1 ounce South African Krugerrands often have a lower premium than 1 ounce gold American Eagles, for example. When you sell gold, of course, you'll get much (but probably not all) of that premium back.

Avoid buying precious metals in the form of old and rare coins unless you want to put in another 20 years of research. The rare coin market often goes up when the bullion market does, but there are a thousand other variables you need to think about when investing. Rare coins are not something you can just swagger in and plunk down your money for, not without getting shafted.

Most important of all, make sure you're having fun and enjoying life. There's no point to hoarding every penny just to die rich. Remember, when you die rich, Uncle Sam is the one who stands the most to gain. Make sure you give yourself a chance to do things you've always wanted to do and to buy a few things you've always had your eye on. You worked hard to earn yourself the choice of what to do with your wealth. Think carefully, enjoy prudently, and take time out for what's truly important to you.

RECOMMENDED READING

I n this book I've just begun to scrape the surface of how you can save money every day. I also haven't really gotten into investment advice, primarily because I'm not really qualified to do so. The following books are some great resources for financial strategies and for the "inside story" on banks and so forth:

Cook, John and Wool, Robert. *All You Need to Know About Banks* (1983). Bantam Books, New York, NY.

Edison, Max. *Beat the Bill Collector* (1997). Paladin Press, Boulder, CO.

Fries, Michael, and Taylor, C. *The Prosperity Handbook* (1984). Communications Research, Oakland, CA.

Kogelman, Stanley, and Heller, Barbara. *The Only Math Book You'll Ever Need* (1994). HarperCollins Publishers, New York, NY.

Mrkvicka, Edward. *The Bank Book* (1989). Harper & Row Publishers, New York, NY.

Pollan, Stephen, and Levine, Mark. *Die Broke* (1997). HarperCollins Publishers, New York, NY.

Tyson, Eric. *Personal Finance for Dummies* (1997). IDG Books Worldwide, Foster City, CA.

If you liked this book, you will also want to read these:

FREE COMPUTERS
A Simple Guide to Building a Working Computer from Scavenged Parts
by James MacLaren

A computer doesn't have to be expensive - in fact, it can be absolutely free! This user-friendly, plain-English guide tells you how to find computers and parts, assemble them and finally understand what makes them work. MacLaren's freestyle approach demystifies the whole process and allows you to build a great system from the ground up. 5 1/2 x 8 1/2, softcover, photos, 176 pp.   **#FREE**

LIVING WELL ON PRACTICALLY NOTHING
Revised and Updated Edition
by Edward H. Romney

If you have been fired, demoted, retired, divorced, widowed or bankrupted, this book is for you. Stocked with proven methods for saving money on shelter, food, clothing, transportation, health care, entertainment and more. Learn to live happily, comfortably and with complete financial freedom – the author has done so since 1969! 8 1/2 x 11, softcover, photos, illus., 200 pp.   **#WELL2**

RAGNAR'S GUIDE TO THE UNDERGROUND ECONOMY
by Ragnar Benson

How would you like to get an immediate 40- to 50-percent raise? You can if you go underground and stop paying taxes. Ragnar shows you how others are cashing in on the underground economy. Find out from them how to pick the right kind of work, get paid in cash, advertise your product or services and prepare a financial statement. *For academic study only.* 5 1/2 x 8 1/2, softcover, photos, 160 pp.   **#ECONOMY**

WEALTH-BUILDING SECRETS AS PRACTICED BY THE WORLD'S RICHEST PEOPLE
What the Kuwaitis Can Teach You about Getting Rich—and Staying Rich
by William Beaver

Do the Kuwaitis have a magic formula for getting rich – besides striking oil? No, but they do have four easy-to-follow secrets that have helped them amass fortunes for centuries – long before oil was discovered. And their secrets will work for you. Guaranteed. 5 1/2 x 8 1/2, softcover, photos, 128 pp.   **#WBS**

BEAT THE BILL COLLECTOR
How to Obtain Freedom from Your Debt
by Max Edison

If debt collection agencies are harassing you to settle your unpaid bills, you do not have to put up with their bullying tactics! This book tells you exactly how you can use simple tricks to get them off your back for good or resort to heavy legal firepower if they persist in calling you at work or home. Know your rights! 5 1/2 x 8 1/2, softcover, 80 pp.   **#BILL**

PALADIN PRESS®

ORDER ONLINE
www.paladin-press.com
RESPONSE CODE: BBK

ORDER TOLL FREE
1.800.392.2400

PHONE: +1.303.443.7250 • FAX: +1.303.442.8741 • E-MAIL: service@paladin-press.com